ALSO BY DAN LYONS

Disrupted: My Misadventure in the Start-Up Bubble

*Lab Rats: How Silicon Valley Made Work Miserable
for the Rest of Us*

STFU

STFU

THE POWER OF KEEPING YOUR MOUTH SHUT

IN AN ENDLESSLY NOISY WORLD

DAN LYONS

HENRY HOLT AND COMPANY

NEW YORK

Henry Holt and Company
Publishers since 1866
120 Broadway
New York, New York 10271
www.henryholt.com

Henry Holt® and ⒣® are registered trademarks of Macmillan Publishing
Group, LLC.

Library of Congress Cataloging-in-Publication Data is available.

ISBN: 9781250850348

Our books may be purchased in bulk for promotional, educational, or
business use. Please contact your local bookseller or the Macmillan Corporate and Premium Sales Department at (800) 221-7945, extension 5442,
or by email at MacmillanSpecialMarkets@macmillan.com.

First Edition 2023

Designed by Omar Chapa

Printed in the United States of America

1   3   5   7   9   10   8   6   4   2

For Sasha, Sonya, and Paul

Is it necessary that every single person on this planet expresses every single opinion that they have on every single thing that occurs, all at the same time? Is that necessary? Or, to ask it a slightly different way, can anyone shut the fuck up? Can any single person shut the fuck up about any single thing for . . . an hour? Is that possible?

—BO BURNHAM, *INSIDE*

CONTENTS

STFU

INTRODUCTION

I'm telling you this as a friend, so please don't take it the wrong way. But I want you to shut the fuck up.

Not for my sake. For yours.

Learning to shut the fuck up will change your life. It will make you smarter, more likable, more creative, and more powerful. It might even help you live longer. People who talk less are more likely to get promoted at work and more likely to prevail in negotiations. Speaking with intention—that is, not just blurting things out—improves our relationships, makes us better parents, and can boost our psychological and even physical well-being. A few years ago, researchers at the University of Arizona discovered that people who spend less time blabbing and devote more time to substantive conversations are happier than everyone else, so much so that having good conversations, they wrote, "might be a key ingredient to a satisfied life."

Failing to shut the fuck up, however, will definitely fuck you up.

Take it from me. I'm an inveterate overtalker, and it

has cost me dearly—in one case, to the tune of millions of dollars. The problem is not only that I talk too much; it's that I have never been able to resist blurting out inappropriate things, and I couldn't keep my opinions to myself. Often I knew even as the words flew out of my mouth that I would regret them and suffer for saying them. But I said them anyway.

Fortunately, for most of my career I worked as a journalist, covering technology for *Forbes* and *Newsweek*. Overtalkers can survive in journalism. In fact, you almost can't do the job unless you are obnoxious enough to say things that people don't want to hear. While working in magazines, I started writing comedy, another field well suited to people who can't keep their mouths shut. I started by writing a blog in which I pretended to be Apple CEO Steve Jobs, which was funny but in a sometimes-off-color way. The blog led to a book deal, which led to a TV development deal, which led to my getting hired as a writer on an HBO comedy, *Silicon Valley*, and all of it led to my being asked to give speeches. The more of a reckless overtalker I became, the better things went.

Of course, karma finally caught up with me. This happened when, figuring I could make a bundle, I talked my way into a marketing role at a software start-up that was headed for an IPO. The start-up offered me a great salary, amazing benefits, and a generous stock option package. The challenge was that, to get all my options, I had to remain employed there for four years. And the corporate world would not tolerate my saltiness.

"You're going to have to bite your tongue—a lot," a journalist friend warned me.

"I know. But I can do it."

"Well, good luck," he said. "But I don't think you'll last a year."

A lot of journalists do manage to make the transition, including some of my friends and former colleagues. If they could do it, why couldn't I? I imagined myself as a contestant on a reality TV show, *Survivor: Start-Up*, where instead of eating bugs, I would have to drink gallons of corporate Kool-Aid and pretend to find it delicious.

I figured the promise of that pot of gold would keep me in line. Instead, I mouthed off about the CEO in an impulsive Facebook post and was voted off the island after twenty months. One day six years later, out of idle curiosity, I looked at the company's stock price, did the math, and discovered to my dismay that if I had lasted four years and held all my shares, they would now have been worth eight million dollars.

That was my costliest disaster, but it was far from the only misfortune I brought upon myself, and not even the worst. At one point, my compulsive overtalking and lack of impulse control led to a separation from my wife, and nearly cost me my marriage. It was then, living alone in a rented house, away from my wife and kids, that I conducted what members of Alcoholics Anonymous call a "searching and fearless moral inventory" of myself, and acknowledged that in ways big and small, overtalking was interfering with my life. This sent me on a search to find the answers to two questions: Why are some people compulsive talkers? And how can we fix it?

This led me to discover something else, which is that all of us, not just overtalkers, stand to gain by talking less, listening more, and communicating with intention. It's a pathway to happiness, a way to make your life immeasurably better. Having set out hoping to learn how to avoid calamities myself, I discovered ideas and developed practices that can make everyone's life better. The problem is not just me. It's not just you. The whole world needs to shut the fuck up.

WE'RE ALL OVERTALKERS

The world is filled with overtalkers. You run into them all the time. They're that pest at the office who destroys every Monday by recounting each completely unremarkable thing they did over the weekend. They're that unself-aware jerk who talks over everyone else at a dinner party while the rest of you fantasize about slipping hemlock into their glass of pinot noir. They're the neighbor who drops in uninvited and spends an hour telling you stories you've already heard, the arrogant know-it-all who interrupts colleagues in meetings, the comedian who blurts out a racist slur and throws away his career, the CEO whose reckless tweet gets him charged with securities fraud.

To be honest, they're most of us, too.

It's not entirely our fault. We live in a world that doesn't just encourage overtalking but practically demands it, where success is measured by how much attention we can attract: get a million Twitter followers, become an Instagram influencer, make a viral video, give a TED Talk. We are inundated with podcasts, YouTube, social media, chat apps, cable TV. Did you know that there are more than 2 million podcasts, which have produced 48 million episodes, and that half those episodes have received fewer than 26 downloads? Or that more than three thousand TEDx events take place every year, with up to twenty wannabe Malcolm Gladwells participating in each one? Or that Americans sit through more than a billion meetings a year, but only 11 percent of them are productive, and half are a complete waste of time? We're tweeting for the sake of tweeting, talking for the sake of talking.

Yet the most powerful and successful people do the exact opposite. Instead of seeking attention, they hold back. When they do speak, they're careful about what they say. Apple CEO Tim Cook lets awkward pauses hang during conversations. Jack Dorsey cofounded Twitter and served as its CEO—but he uses it sparingly. Even Richard Branson, a relentless showman and self-promoter, extols the virtues of being a shutter-upper in meetings. Albert Einstein hated the telephone and avoided it as much as possible. The late Supreme Court justice Ruth Bader Ginsburg chose her words so carefully and took such painfully long pauses that her clerks developed a habit they called "the Two-Mississippi Rule": Finish what you're saying and then count "One Mississippi . . . two Mississippi" before you speak again. The justice was not ignoring you; she was thinking . . . very . . . deeply . . . about how to respond. One of RBG's most famous bits of advice was that, in a marriage and in the workplace, "It helps sometimes to be a little deaf."

Talk less, get more. This book is about learning how to engage with the world in ways that give us an advantage. We may not get appointed to the Supreme Court or become tech billionaires, but we can prevail in our own day-to-day battles. Buying a new car or house? Hoping to move up the ladder at work? Trying to win friends and influence people? Learn how to shut the fuck up.

In the entirety of human history there has never been such a noisy age, and it keeps getting noisier. We're not wired for such constant overstimulation, and it's hurting our brains—literally causing brain damage—and straining our cardiovascular systems. We're triggered, angry, juiced with cortisol, and a little bit off our rockers. The road to recovery begins with bailing out of the noise tornado. Better yet, by learning how to STFU we can improve not only our own lives but also the lives of the people around us— our kids, spouses, friends, and colleagues. In the grandest sense, we can make the whole world a better place if we all turn down the volume a little bit.

Oddly enough, it's not so easy to do.

FIVE WAYS TO STFU

Shutting up should be the easiest thing in the world. All you have to do is nothing, right? But, in fact, not talking requires a lot of concentration. It's probably more difficult than talking. Have you ever spent time in a foreign country where you speak a little of the local language but not well enough for it to feel natural, so that in every conversation, even simple ones, your brain is constantly working overtime to translate from the local language to your native tongue and then back again? By the end of the day, you're exhausted. That's what it feels like at first when you start concentrating on the way you speak. It's draining. For an overtalker like me, it can be almost painful.

The trick is to start slow. Instead of making one big change, you make a bunch of little ones. I approach STFU as a daily practice, like meditation or yoga. Just as with meditation we force ourselves to become conscious of our breathing, I force myself to become conscious of how I am speaking. I lower my voice, slow my cadence, and take . . . long . . . pauses.

My search for solutions has been one of trial and error, using myself as a test subject. From research and interviews with experts, I have developed five practices that I think of as a kind of workout. The point isn't to do all of them at once, or even to do one of them for an entire day. You don't spend sixteen hours a day in the gym, right? These are exercises. Pick one and use it during a thirty-minute Zoom call. Or when you're in the car with your spouse. Or sitting at the breakfast table with your teenager.

Some you will like more than others. Some you will find useful; others not so much. That's fine. Take whatever works for you.

Here are my Five Ways to STFU:

When possible, say nothing. Early twentieth-century humorist Will Rogers once said you should never miss a good chance to shut up. You will be shocked by how many good chances there are. Pretend words are money, and spend them wisely. Be Dirty Harry, not Jim Carrey.

Master the power of the pause. Copy the trick invented by RBG's law clerks who trained themselves to wait two seconds before they spoke. Take a breath. Pause. Let the other person process what you've just said. Learn to wield the power of the pause.

Quit social media. The first cousin of overtalking is overtweeting, and it is almost impossible not to fall into the trap. Platforms like Facebook and Twitter are designed to get you addicted. If you can't quit completely, at least dial it way back.

Seek out silence. Noise makes us sick. Literally. Information overload makes us constantly agitated and overstimulated, which leads to health problems and can even shorten our lives. Detach. Unplug. Spend time without your phone. Don't talk, don't read, don't watch, don't listen. Giving your brain a rest can kick-start your creativity and make you healthier and more productive. Research suggests silence might even help us grow brain cells.

Learn how to listen. Being a great listener is considered such an important business skill that CEOs go to boot camps to learn how to do it. And it's hard work, because listening should be an active endeavor rather than a passive one. Instead of just *hearing* someone, active listening means blocking out everything else and paying fierce attention to what the other person is saying. Nothing makes people happier than the feeling of being authentically heard and seen.

YOU WON'T BELIEVE WHAT HAPPENS NEXT

I can't always maintain this discipline, but when I do, the results are magical. I feel calmer, less anxious, and more in control, which makes me less likely to overtalk. It's a positive feedback loop. The less I talk, the less I talk.

Better yet, I see the effect on the people around me. My teenage daughter and I sit on the porch in the evening and have long conversations filled with laughter. If you are the parent of a high school–age kid, you know how miraculous this feels. She tells me her dreams and what she thinks she might want to do with her life. She tells me about her fears and doubts. Instead of trying to solve her problems, I listen. Inevitably, she works her way around to solving them herself and concludes that she is going to be all right and that she knows what she needs to do. I discover that she has never felt confident playing Mozart and Haydn on the piano and that, now that she is going to a summer camp, where she will have to play Haydn in a trio, she's freaking out. She fears she might not be able to do it, but at the same time, she would rather try and fail than chicken out. I discover that she is sometimes terrified to go to French class because she signed up for a course that's too hard for her and for which she probably won't get an A, but that she will probably learn more by having to struggle with the material. I discover that I don't just admire her, but that I'm inspired by her.

Learning to STFU means pushing back against a world that encourages us to talk more, not less. In this book, I describe ways to do that. I explain how STFU can be applied at home, at work, and in matters of the heart—dating and relationships. You will learn how to talk less and become more powerful, and how becoming a great listener will transform your life.

My nonpatented STFU Method is a practice, not a miracle cure. It won't help you lose twenty pounds, look ten years younger, or get rich without lifting a finger. But it will help you become a little bit happier, a little bit healthier, a little more successful. You will still catch yourself getting excited and talking too much. This happens to me all the time. It's okay. We're human. We slip up. But tomorrow we will do better.

I'm hoping you will finish this book feeling inspired to make changes in your life—and armed with a road map for getting there.

THE TALKAHOLIC SCALE

When I first set out to fix my problem with overtalking, I discovered that communication researchers have defined a condition called "talkaholism," a form of extreme, compulsive overtalking that is akin to an addiction. They created the following self-scored questionnaire to identify people who suffer from the condition. Answer the sixteen questions and then consult the instructions at the end to calculate your score. To double-check your results, ask someone who knows you to answer the same questions about you and calculate their score. Be warned: this might get awkward.

THE TALKAHOLIC SCALE

DIRECTIONS: This questionnaire includes sixteen statements about talking behavior. Please indicate the degree to which you believe that each of these characteristics applies to you by marking on the line before each item whether you (5) strongly agree that it applies, (4) agree that it applies, (3) are undecided, (2) disagree that it applies, or (1) strongly disagree that it applies. There are no right or wrong answers. Work quickly; record your first impression.

_____ 1. Often I keep quiet when I know I should talk.

_____ 2. I talk more than I should sometimes.

_____ 3. Often I talk when I should keep quiet.

_____ 4. Sometimes I keep quiet when I know it would be to my advantage to talk.

_____ 5. I am a "talkaholic."

_____ 6. Sometimes I feel compelled to keep quiet.

_____ 7. In general, I talk more than I should.

_____ 8. I am a compulsive talker.

_____ 9. I am *not* a talker; rarely do I talk in communication situations.

_____ 10. Quite a few people have said I talk too much.

_____ 11. I just can't stop talking too much.

_____ 12. In general, I talk less than I should.

_____ 13. I am *not* a "talkaholic."

_____ 14. Sometimes I talk when it would be to my advantage to keep quiet.

_____ 15. I talk less than I should sometimes.

_____ 16. I am *not* a compulsive talker.

SCORING: To determine your score, complete the following steps:

Step 1. Add the scores for items 2, 3, 5, 7, 8, 10, 11, and 14.

Step 2. Add the scores for items 13 and 16.

Step 3. Complete the following formula:

Talkaholic score = 12 + (total from Step 1) − (total from Step 2).

Items 1, 4, 6, 9, 12, and 15 are filler items and are not scored.
Your score should be between 10 and 50.
Most people score below 30.
People who score between 30 and 39 are borderline talkaholics and can control their talking most of the time, but sometimes they find themselves in situations where it is difficult to be quiet, even if it would be very much to their advantage not to talk.
People with scores above 40 are talkaholics.

Reprinted with permission of Virginia Richmond.

1

WHAT WE TALK ABOUT WHEN WE TALK ABOUT OVERTALKING

I got 50 points on the Talkaholic Scale, the highest possible score. My wife, Sasha, gave me the same 50 points and probably wished she could give me more. This was not unexpected, but according to the researchers who developed the test this might be cause for concern. They described talkaholism as an addiction akin to alcoholism and said that while a talkaholic's gift with words can help them advance in their careers, their inability to rein in their overtalking often leads to personal and professional setbacks. Check, check, and check.

Talkaholics cannot just wake up one day and choose to talk less. Their talking is compulsive. They don't talk just a little bit more than everyone else, but a lot more, and they do this all the time, in every context or setting, even when they know that other people think they talk too much. And here is the gut punch: Talkaholics continue to talk even when they know that what they are about to say is going to hurt them. They simply cannot stop.

"That's me," I said to Sasha. "Right? That's totally me."

"I've been telling you this for years," she said.

We were sitting in the kitchen. The kids—twins, a boy and a girl, fifteen years old—weren't home. Memories flew around in my brain, times when I blurted out something off-color at a party, or embarrassed the kids by talking someone's ear off, or regaled them with a long story I had told a thousand times before. "Danalogues," we called them, and we would all laugh and pretend it was funny— "You know how Dad loves to talk!" But now, looking at these test results in black-and-white, I didn't feel like laughing. I felt embarrassed. And concerned.

I didn't know how or where to get help, but I decided to begin by tracking down the two researchers who created the Talkaholic Scale, figuring they might have some advice. They were a husband-and-wife team, Virginia Richmond and James C. McCroskey, who had taught at West Virginia University. McCroskey, who was something of a legend in the field of communication studies, died in 2012, but Richmond, who is retired, lives in a little town outside Charleston, West Virginia.

The two got interested in studying talkaholics for one simple reason: "Because my husband was one," Richmond told me. They were an odd pair. McCroskey was the life of the party, while Richmond was and still is painfully shy—or "communicatively apprehensive," as researchers say. "We wanted to figure out why some people talk so much and some people talk hardly at all. There was a lot of literature about people who did not talk much, but not much had been done about people at the other end, the compulsive talkers." Some researchers believed there was no such thing as a person who talks too much, and that when we say that someone talks too much, what we really mean is that they are saying things we don't want to hear. Richmond and McCroskey insisted that this was ridiculous, that of course there were people who absolutely talked too much—"We knew them," Richmond says—and that, what's more, there were some people who were not just talkative but whose compulsion to talk was akin to an addiction. "That's why we came up with the name 'talkaholics,'" Richmond told me.

The couple created the Talkaholic Scale to see if talkaholics could be identified. If so, researchers might be able to develop ways to help them. "We didn't think there would be very many," Richmond said, but when they gave the Talkaholic Scale to eight hundred students at West Virginia University, they found that 5 percent qualified as talkaholics—which, oddly enough, is about the same percentage as that of alcoholics in the general population.

I explained to Richmond that I had reached out to her because I had scored a 50 on the Talkaholic Scale, and wanted to learn what causes compulsive talking and how it can be fixed. Richmond had bad news and more bad news. First, she and her husband had never figured out what causes talkaholism. Worse, while they had found ways to help communicatively apprehensive people come out of their shell, they had come to believe that talkaholics were beyond help. "We used to joke that you can't keep a good talkaholic down," she said with a laugh. "There's no remedy. You can't cure a talkaholic."

Still, she said, she and her husband did their work thirty years ago. Other people have been pursuing the subject since then. The best, she said, was Michael Beatty, a professor who once worked with Richmond and McCroskey and now teaches at the University of Miami. Beatty apparently developed an interest in talkaholics for the same reason McCroskey had: "He's the biggest talkaholic I've ever known," she told me. "You can tell him I said that. He won't take it as an insult."

Beatty is kind of eccentric. He doesn't own a smartphone and does not keep a personal computer in his home. To reach him, you have to send an email to his university address and wait for him to go into the office to check his mail, which takes as long as it takes. My talk with Richmond left me a little bit disheartened, but I remained hopeful that Beatty might offer some help or advice. So, one day, I wrote him an email, pressed Send, and waited.

THE MAD LIFE OF A TALKAHOLIC

For a long time, I deluded myself into believing that I was just a gregarious, outgoing guy who liked to have great conversations. I talked to anyone and everyone: Uber drivers, strangers on chairlifts, "and every waiter and waitress you ever met," Sasha says. But eventually I started becoming aware that I had a problem, because even when I tried to talk less, I couldn't. I dreaded social events. Neighborhood barbecues and birthday parties were excruciating. It was like riding a pogo stick across a minefield. I would try to mingle, the whole time thinking, *Don't talk too much don't talk too much don't talk too much*. But even when I prepared myself, I sometimes found myself going off the rails, monologuing like Hamlet on crystal meth.

Eventually, in desperation, I resorted to a brute force approach and began pregaming with Ativan, a drug used to treat anxiety. I would arrive to parties in a wonderful, fuzzy benzodiazepine haze and quietly slip away to some nook where I could zone out by myself and watch TV or read my Twitter feed until it was time to go home. The neighbors thought I was rude or weird—or, as one told my wife, "Dan's a little bit . . . crazy, you know?" From my perspective, I believed I was doing them a favor by drugging myself into a stupor to avoid annoying them with my overtalking.

The amazing thing is that, even dosed up on benzos, I would sometimes talk too much or say something awkward or stupid. As soon as we left a party I would ask Sasha, "Did I talk too much?" Too often, her answer was yes.

As I became aware of my own problem, I started recognizing it in other people. There was our next-door neighbor, an education consultant who was lively and loud and could take over a room like no one I'd ever met. (I adored her; other neighbors did not.) There was the smartest-person-in-the-room management consultant who loved the sound of his own booming voice. There was the scientist who did not suffer fools gladly, and who paid the price for it. There was the lonely retired financial adviser who would show up around dinnertime, make himself comfortable at the kitchen counter, and settle in for a soliloquy on the latest happenings in the S&P 500. There was the artist who would call and keep me on the phone for an hour or more, telling me the same stories again and again. (As a mutual friend put it, "You don't talk to him; you listen.") And there was my mother-in-law, a nonnative English speaker, who machine-gunned us with bad grammar, mutilated sentences, and pronouns unmoored from their antecedents and who never took her finger off the trigger; sometimes we literally had to shout to interrupt her.

We overtalkers seem to be drawn to one another, probably because we're the only people who can put up with us. In any setting, we are quick to recognize one of our kind, the way vampires and serial killers do. Sometimes two of us will hole up and overtalk together, yapping for hours, never running out of things to say—indulging our addiction, interrupting each other, reveling in the joy of gabbing away with someone who understands us, in a setting where we won't be judged or punished. It's our safe space. Pure bliss.

Undertalkers, however, drive us out of our minds. They annoy us as much as we annoy them. We feel about undertalkers the way your dog feels about you when you won't throw him a tennis ball to fetch. *Come on, man! Come on!*

One thing compulsive overtalkers have in common is that sooner or later most of us get kneecapped. There is no escaping it. Tony Soprano said guys in his line of work had only two ways out, death or prison. Overtalkers similarly know that, one day, our talking will catch up with us. Some of us become high achievers, but a lot of us become serial screwups, our lives a string of fiascos, disasters, and catastrophes.

A longtime friend is a very bright guy with an Ivy League degree, but compulsive talking has cost him jobs because (a) he could not resist telling his colleagues that they were dimwits; and (b) they usually did not appreciate his candor. "I'll just snap," he says. "I'll be in some dumb meeting, thinking, *Why am I in this stupid meeting?* Then I'll flip out and start explaining to all of them why they're fucking morons, even though I know that the smart move

would be to keep quiet. I can always be counted on to say
the wrong thing, and the worst part is, I know it even while
I'm doing it. And then I immediately regret it. But, at that
point, there's no walking it back."

Overtalkers are universally hated. Look at the words
used to describe us: *gasbag, windbag, motormouth, prat-
tler, blatherskite.* We say someone has "verbal diarrhea" or
"talks a lot of shit." In the United Kingdom and Ireland,
they call you a "gobshite" (which combines *gob*, "mouth,"
and *shite*, "shit") or a "shitehawk," someone who rains
down shit from above. In Italy, they say that someone
attacca un bottone—that is, talks so long you could sew on
a button. Or, *mi ha attaccato un pippone*—which translates roughly as doing something gross into someone's ear.
Italians might call you a *trombone*, which sounds really
cool with an Italian accent, or a *quaquaraquà*, an ono-
matopoeic Sicilian slang word for someone who talks a lot
but is an idiot. In Brazil, they say *fala mais que o homem
do rádio*—"he talks more than the man on the radio." In
Spain, you're a *bocachancla*, a "flip-flop mouth"; and in the
Spanish province of Catalonia, you're a *bocamoll*, a "loose
mouth." In Germany, overtalkers are *Plappermäuler*, which
combines *plapper*, "to babble," and *maul*, a coarse term
describing an animal's mouth. Russians, who can always be
relied upon to deliver the filthiest way to say anything, call
overtalkers *pizdaboly*, a nasty term that combines *pizda*, an
extremely obscene word for female genitalia, and *bol*, the
root for the verb "to flap." Ugh.

The Japanese, who treasure silence and can't stand
noisy people, have a proverb: "If the bird had not sung, it
would not have been shot." In India, they tell a children's

story about a *batuni kachua* (talkative tortoise) whose overtalking leads to ruin. When a drought strikes and the pond
dries up, two geese offer to carry the talkative tortoise to
another lake. The geese carry a stick between them, and
the tortoise hangs on to it by his mouth. Of course, the tortoise can't resist the urge to talk, and as soon as he opens his
mouth, he loses his grip and hurtles to earth, where he gets
smashed to death on some rocks and/or eaten by villagers.

This is how people view overtalkers. They fantasize
about our deaths.

SIX KINDS OF OVERTALKERS

After talking to Richmond, I began diving into the research
about compulsive speech, and discovered that there are different kinds of overtalking. There's *hyperverbal speech*,
where you can't help interrupting people (your brain is
revved up, and you're talking a mile a minute); *disorga-
nized speech*, where you leap from one unrelated subject to
another; and *situational overtalking*, which pretty much
everyone has experienced at one time or another. I'm sure
you can look back, usually with a cringe, and remember
times when you should have talked less. Have you ever
blurted out something that hurt someone's feelings? Told
a joke that offended someone? Last time you bought a car,
when the salesperson stopped talking and let an awkward
silence hang in the air, did you rush in to fill the void? I'll
bet you did—and it cost you money. Maybe you talked too
much in a sales call and lost the deal—and your commission along with it. Maybe you interrupted someone in a
meeting, and your boss, down at the other end of the table,
noticed this and began to form a poor impression of you.

She might not even have realized that her perception of you shifted, but eight months later, the promotion you were hoping to win went to someone else.

Just as there are different kinds of overtalking, there are different kinds of overtalkers. I put them into six categories:

- *Ego Talkers* are the loud-voiced, know-it-all guys (and, yes, they're almost always guys) who interrupt people and dominate conversations because they honestly believe their ideas are better than everyone else's, even when they don't know what they're talking about. Silicon Valley, where I've spent a lot of my career, teems with guys (and they are always guys) who have made a fortune in software and now know everything about everything. Climate change? Heart surgery? Bitcoin Man knows more than the experts.

- *Nervous Talkers* struggle with social anxiety and babble to self-soothe.

- *Ruminators* do their thinking out loud—they talk to themselves, basically—and annoy everyone around them.

- *Blurters* are highly verbal and quick thinkers, but they lack a filter.

- *Blabbers* spout nonsense, tell the same stories over and over, and keep going even when you try to interrupt them, like a car with no brakes hurtling down a hill.

- *Talkaholics*, the most extreme offenders, are compulsive and self-destructive.

In the past decade or so, researchers have started to get a handle on the causes of overtalking—some of them psychological and some biological. Some overtalkers are just extroverts; it's their innate personality type. Sometimes overtalking is caused by social anxiety. (That's often the case with Blurters, Blabbers, and Nervous Talkers.) But extreme, compulsive talking—the kind that makes you a talkaholic—can indicate deeper psychological issues, like narcissistic personality disorder. So-called pressured speech—loud, rapid, unstoppable—can be caused by hypomania, which is an indication of bipolar II, the milder form of the disorder. Overtalking may also indicate someone has attention-deficit/hyperactivity disorder (ADHD).

If you scored high on the Talkaholic Scale, consider seeing a professional to get an evaluation. The good news is that, these days, things like ADHD and bipolar II disorder can be treated with meds and therapy. The meds don't cure you, but they can tamp down the noise in your brain so that you can work on your issues in therapy. For what it's worth, overtalkers *love* therapy.

I was still slogging through piles of research papers, and still not finding any great answers, when one day I checked my email and got a surprise. Michael Beatty from the University of Miami had written back, saying that he would love to talk to me and that, in fact, after many years and countless experiments, he had figured out what causes talkaholism.

THE CALLS ARE COMING FROM INSIDE YOUR BRAIN

"It's biology," Beatty told me when we got on the phone. "It's all nature, not nurture. It starts to develop prenatally."

Twenty years ago, Beatty pioneered a field called "communibiology," which studies communication as a biological phenomenon. Instead of teaching courses in journalism and public speaking, the traditional business of a university communication department, he collaborated with neuroscientists, giving study participants EEGs to measure their brain waves and sticking them into fMRI machines to watch their brains light up when they looked at pictures or listened to audio recordings.

A lot of communication researchers thought he was going down a blind alley, but Beatty was sure he was right. "To me, it would be weird if the way we communicate was *not* related to the brain," he said. "We just didn't know how." In 2011, Beatty and his colleagues at the University of Miami discovered that talkativeness is determined by brain wave imbalances. Specifically, it's about the balance between neuron activity in the left and right lobes in the anterior region of the prefrontal cortex. Ideally, the left and right lobe should have about the same amount of neuronal activity when a person is at rest. If there's an asymmetry—if one side lights up more than the other—you end up being an above-average or below-average talker. If your left side is more active than the right, you're shy. If the right side is more active, you're talkative. The greater the imbalance, the farther out on the talkativeness spectrum you will be. A talkaholic's right lobe will fire like crazy while the left side barely flickers.

"It's all about impulse control," Beatty told me. Imbalances in the anterior cortex also relate to aggression and to "your ability to assess how a plan might unfold and what the consequences will be." Extreme right-side activity "shows up a lot in spousal murder," he said.

I did not mention this to my wife.

The right-dominant lack of impulse control often plays out in the workplace. "If I'm right-side dominant and I'm a CEO, and I'm in a meeting where some employee starts saying dumb things, I'm not going to be polite. I'm going to get angry and tell him to shut up," Beatty said.

Unfortunately, a talkaholic can't become a non-talkaholic, Beatty says. After all, you can't rewire your brain or zap your neurons back into balance. "It's not completely deterministic, but there's very little room to change who you are," he told me.

SI SE PUEDE STFU

For four decades, Joe Biden was the reigning champ of blowing himself up on the campaign trail—newspapers crowned him the King of Gaffes. But somehow in 2020, Biden developed the discipline to STFU. He kept his voice low and his answers short. He paused before speaking. When reporters showed up, he took only a few questions, gave boring answers, and then bolted.

Biden's story gave me hope. I figured that if he could train himself to STFU, surely I could, too. I had no dreams of running for public office, but I had plenty of motivation. I wanted to be a better spouse, parent, and friend. I wanted to stop dreading social events. There might be no cure for talkaholism, but there's also no cure for alcoholism, yet some alcoholics develop the discipline to stop drinking.

I couldn't afford a speech coach. I couldn't find any online courses that teach you how to STFU. So, after talking to Beatty, I struck out on my own, interviewing dozens of people who, in one way or another, are experts on speech: historians, social scientists, political scientists, communication professors, executive coaches, psychologists. I went forest bathing in the Berkshires with a guide. I took an online listening course, and got tips from a professor who teaches courses in listening. A psychologist in California shared with me the techniques she teaches to prisoners to help them STFU during parole hearings and non-talk their way out of prison—methods that I hoped would help me break free from the metaphorical prison that overtalking had built around me.

Armed with theory, advice, and exercises, I developed my "Five Ways to STFU" and started practicing them. I thought of it as a daily workout. I bailed out of social media almost entirely. I trained myself to become comfortable with uncomfortable silences. Before picking up the phone or getting on a Zoom call, I took deep breaths to slow myself down, using the heart rate monitor on my Apple Watch to see whether this was working. During the call, I would lower my voice and slow my cadence. I asked my kids open-ended questions, then sat back and let them speak. Officially speaking, we were "having a talk," but in truth, I was having a listen.

I attached a piece of paper to the wall above my computer screen with admonishments in 60-point type: "QUIET!

LISTEN! SHORT ANSWERS! WRAP IT UP!" One of my overtalking friends keeps a note taped to her laptop that reads, "God, help me keep my mouth shut." Before meetings, I took a moment to think through the purpose of the call: what I needed to convey and what I needed to learn. I wrote those down on a notepad and stuck to the talking points.

Gradually, I began to develop more discipline, and as I did, something extraordinary happened: I began to feel better, both emotionally and physically. I felt happier. I was nicer to people. They seemed nicer to me. Life felt easier.

That's when I realized that STFU can do more than just help you avoid calamities or haggle a better price on a car—that, in fact, STFU is a kind of therapy.

THE ANXIETY WHEEL

Anxiety is the theme song of our age. Rates were already rising in the United States before Covid-19, especially among young people, and then they soared during the pandemic lockdown. In 2019, two-thirds of Americans said they were extremely or somewhat anxious, according to the American Psychiatric Association. One in five American adults suffers from a full-blown anxiety disorder.

Overtalkers talk to relieve anxiety, or distract ourselves from feeling it. But instead of relieving anxiety, overtalking makes it worse. The more you talk, the more anxious you become. It's a vicious circle. I call it the Anxiety Wheel.

The same thing happens on social media. We use sites like Facebook, Instagram, TikTok, and Twitter as soothing mechanisms. Feeling anxious, we open an app and start scrolling, hoping to push the anxiety away. But, again, the opposite happens. In your attempt to mitigate anxiety, you instead only compound it. Once again, you're on the Anxiety Wheel.

If you can resist the urge to talk, and force yourself not to pick up your phone, you can start rolling the Anxiety Wheel backward, in the opposite direction. Sitting in silence feels awful at first, but if you can sit with the discomfort, it will begin to wane. Doctors have found that, for some people, quitting social media has the same effect as taking an antidepressant.

STFU AS PERSONAL TRANSFORMATION

How we speak is who we are. It's how we define ourselves, and shapes the way we perceive others. When you try to explain what someone is like, how do you do it? What is your assessment based on? Usually you define their personality by describing the way they speak. Fast talker or slow talker? Quiet or loud? Talkative or taciturn? Our speech is how we reveal our personality to the world. In a way, the way we speak *is* our personality. If you change the way you speak, you are in effect changing yourself.

Talking is like breathing. You don't think about it; you just do it. When you start paying attention to *how* you speak, this leads you to think about *why* you speak the way you do. You're forcing yourself to become conscious of something that usually happens unconsciously. Now you're doing the kind of work you might do with meditation or psychotherapy. You're turning your attention inward. You're engaging in self-reflection and self-examination. You're figuring out who you are.

STFU is not just a workout. It's also a psychological

process, an active, dynamic practice. Anything that requires effort, focus, practice, and mental discipline can transform you and define you. Martial arts work that way for some people. For others it's mastering the piano, playing chess, gardening, cooking.

I used to be a rower. It's a sport that requires a mix of physical and mental strength, and the mental part may be the more important of the two. Rowing requires total concentration every second—keeping the boat balanced, thinking about your hands, feeling the pull of the blade through the water, timing the drive and recovery. It's repetitive. You do the same thing again and again, with each stroke trying to achieve perfection and rarely achieving that. The hour or two that you spend on the water every day becomes as much a Zen meditation as it is a workout. It defines you. That's why rowers sometimes say, "I row," but they more often say, "I'm a rower."

When I began, I just wanted to stop stumbling into calamities and annoying other people. But I ended up taking a journey of self-discovery. STFU became a pathway to personal change and transformation.

2

SITFO: SHUT IT THE FUCK OFF

The internet has given us more ways to talk than ever before—so we use them. How many apps do you have on your phone to communicate with people? How many in-boxes do you check? Most likely you have work email, personal email, and text messages. On top of that, maybe Slack, Facebook, Twitter, Instagram, LinkedIn, WhatsApp, Telegram, or Signal—and those are just the popular ones.

We talk to our TVs and remote controls. We talk to gizmos in our living rooms, to our lightbulbs and thermostats, to our watches, to bots, to the dashboards in our cars—and some of these things talk back to us. We jabber on our phones in places that once were sanctuaries for silence: in the car, in the woods. We huff and puff through conversations while we're out for a jog or working out at the gym. We whip out our phones at movies, concerts, funerals: no place is sacred. The worst humans among us engage in Asshole Talking: yakking into their phones in public places (trains, restaurants, coffee shops) while everyone around them fumes. Two-thirds of us use phones when we're in the bathroom, while 20 percent bring phones into the shower, and 10 percent have even checked their phone while having sex.

When we're not talking, we're consuming—drinking from a fire hose of information that is mostly just noise wearing a disguise. Netflix will release *eighty-seven* movies in 2022, plus forty shows and a few specials. That's about six hundred hours of video, and the streaming platform will spend $17 billion to produce it all. On top of that, we have Apple TV+, Amazon Prime Video, Disney Plus, HBO, Hulu, Starz—on and on—plus the regular old movie studios and TV networks churning out sitcoms, rom-coms, and superhero comic book movies in which, every week, the world faces a new threat of extinction before being rescued by someone in skintight clothing.

In 2022, there were 817,000 unique titles available on streaming services, and this, according to Nielsen, was "prompting growing confusion." Nearly half of people feel overwhelmed by so many choices, Nielsen found. Yet we keep consuming more. In the twelve months ending in February 2022, Americans watched 169.4 billion minutes of streaming content *each week*, a gain of 18 percent from the year before. All told, Americans consumed 15 million years' worth of streaming video in 2021. A survey in 2022 found that the average American will watch 290 movies and TV shows in 2022—that's 437 hours, equivalent to eighteen full days. By 2020, we were spending four times as much money on streaming services as we did in 2015.

We are surrounded by noise pollution, immersed in a relentless cacophony. No indoor space is allowed to be free of music—it's the law, apparently. Sound levels in restau-

rants and spin classes have been measured at over 100 decibels. That's as loud as a jackhammer. The problem is not
just the loudness; it's that there's no escape. A few years
ago, it emerged that the United States tortured prisoners at
Abu Ghraib and Guantánamo Bay by blasting endless loops
of loud music, including, notably, the *Barney* theme song.
If you're a parent, you understand why that would work.
Now restaurants, shopping malls, department stores, and
even hospitals have taken a page from the torturer's play-
book, and it is taking a toll. Every study about open-office
floor plans finds that noise destroys our ability to think
straight and get work done. Endlessly looping Christmas
music is such torment that retail workers in Austria went
on strike to force their employers to stop playing it. "People feel powerless," says Nigel Rodgers, a curmudgeonly
Brit who founded Pipedown, a group whose members have
successfully driven retailers and restaurants in the UK to
banish background music. "You go to the doctor and they
tell you your blood pressure is high, and you say, 'Well it
wasn't when I came in here, it's that awful music blaring in
your waiting room.'"

We spend our lives attached to screens: smartphones,
tablets, laptops, TVs. Tesla owners can play video games
and watch movies on their dashboard screen because . . .
why not? We put screens in elevators, on gym equipment,
on refrigerators, on gas pumps, on the walls above urinals.
Ski areas put digital displays on chairlifts and blast music
in gondolas, because why gaze in silent, childlike wonder
at majestic snowcapped peaks when you can rock out to
Metallica? Google developed glasses to fire information
into our eyeballs, which failed, but Apple is rumored to be

working on something similar, and theirs will probably succeed because they will look cool and be wildly overpriced—catnip for the Apple faithful. Facebook's parent company, Meta, sells virtual reality goggles that attach the screen directly to your face and is building an imaginary world called the metaverse, where we will meta-work, meta-shop, buy meta-houses, have meta-sex, and go meta-mental. If Mark Zuckerberg gets his way, we might spend more time online than in the real world.

We don't just need to STFU. We need to SITFO: Shut It the Fuck Off.

WE HAVE MET THE ENEMY, AND IT IS US

The great thing about the internet is that it made it possible—and easy and cheap—for anyone to create anything and share it online. The bad thing is that so many people have availed themselves of this opportunity. There are now more than 600 million blogs on the internet, spewing out 29 million new posts every day. There are 2 million podcasts, four times as many as in 2018, and for the most part nobody is listening to them. Thousands of people spend millions of dollars (all told) to attend conferences hosted by organizations like the Global Speakers Federation and the National Speakers Association, where you sit in a darkened auditorium watching public speakers speaking publicly about the art of public speaking to people who dream of being public speakers. Why? Thanks to TED, and its hellspawn stepchild TEDx, each year tens of thousands of would-be life coaches, thought leaders, and public intellectuals get to stand on a stage wearing a silly headset microphone and inform the rest of us that if we could just double down on ourselves, operationalize our values, own our stories, map meaningful connections, and make stress our friend, we might stumble into happiness. I would rather stumble into a pool of fire. Every minute, 500 hours of new video content gets uploaded to YouTube. In the same sixty seconds, roughly 1.8 million Snaps are created, and 700,000 stories are posted on Instagram. Nearly 600,000 tweets are tweeted, 150,000 Slack messages sent. Each minute, people watch 167 million TikTok videos, 4.1 million YouTube videos, 70,000 hours of Netflix content, and listen to 40,000 hours of music on Spotify.

Every. Damn. Minute.

Comedian Bo Burnham wonders in *Inside*, a special he shot at home during the Covid-19 lockdown, "Is it necessary that every single person on this planet expresses every single opinion that they have on every single thing that occurs, all at the same time? Is that necessary? Or, to ask it a slightly different way, can anyone shut the fuck up? Can any single person shut the fuck up about any single thing for . . . an hour? Is that possible?"

The Cambrian explosion of content began in the early 2000s, when the internet became speedy enough to be useful. But it really took off in the 2010s, when the smartphone came along, enabling us to carry infinite forms of distraction in our pockets wherever we went and to remain connected at all times. In the days of dial-up modems, we used to talk about "getting on the internet." Now the internet is on us. We carry it on our bodies. The internet is ambient, and because of that, work demands that we be available at all times, fielding emails and getting pinged on Slack. On an average weekday, Slack racks up more than one billion usage minutes. Having originated as a lifeline for workers, especially those who work remotely, the platform too often becomes a way for those annoying pests who used to interfere with your work by sticking their heads into your office to do the same thing to you in the virtual world.

The average American uses ten apps a day, thirty apps per month, and checks their smartphone every 12 minutes. Hardcore addicts check their phones every 4 minutes. One out of five Millennials opens an app *more than fifty times a day*. In 2010, people in the United States used their smartphones for 24 minutes a day on average. By 2021, that rose to 4 hours and 23 minutes per day. TikTok has more than a billion users, and according to one research firm, the average user spends 850 minutes on the app *per month*.

We are such gluttons for content punishment that we play YouTube videos and podcasts at double speed so that we can get through them faster. Even that's not enough, so we look at multiple screens at the same time. We binge-watch *Ted Lasso* while scrolling through Twitter, TikTok, and Instagram on our iPhones and checking email on our laptops. About 90 percent of us look at a second device while watching TV. Why do we do it? Because we can.

The problem is, we can't. Our brains suck at multitasking. Trying to do it makes us dumber—literally. One study found that multitasking lowered people's IQ to the level of an eight-year-old's or of someone who had stayed up all night smoking weed. Take your pick. Researchers have identified a disorder called "digital amnesia," an inability to accumulate long-term memories. In one survey, 40 percent of participants could not remember their children's phone numbers or the phone number for their place of work.

Meanwhile, the content we consume keeps getting shorter, which lays waste to our ability to sustain focus. In 2015, a Microsoft research team made the shocking discovery that since the year 2000, the average human attention span had dropped from twelve seconds to eight seconds, which is shorter than that of a goldfish. This was *before* TikTok came along to pump fifteen-second clips at us while we stare at our phones, gape-jawed and mesmerized. By now, our attention span must have plunged to . . . what? Four seconds? That still puts us ahead of fruit flies, which have an attention span of less than one second, but we'll find a way to get there.

GARBAGE AT THE SPEED OF LIGHT

The problem is not just how much stuff is flying at us but also that so much of the stuff is brain-melting digital dog shit. What some people call the (second) Golden Age of Television began in 1999 with *The Sopranos*, followed by *Mad Men*, *Breaking Bad*, and *Game of Thrones*. You can argue—people do—about whether that golden age has ended, is fizzling out, or is still going strong. What you can't argue about is that for every good show, there are fifty awful ones, and soon there will be one hundred. We are surrounded by an ocean of toxic waste, and sea levels are rising.

Jake Paul brays like a brain-damaged donkey . . . and has twenty million YouTube subscribers. Dr. Pimple Popper machine-guns blackheads and volcanoes of pus at our screens . . . and has been running seven seasons. Johnny Knoxville has made five Jackass movies, which basically consist of imbeciles inventing new ways to smash one another in the balls . . . and those movies have grossed more than five hundred million dollars at the box office. The noisier things get, the more outrageous, offensive, and obnoxious you must be to stand out. The result is a world that has become a cross between *Jerry Springer* and *Idiocracy*, a movie about a dystopian future where humans have devolved into morons and the most popular TV show is *Ow! My Balls!*, which is about . . . well, yeah.

If there *is* some superior alien civilization tracking us from a zillion light years away, they probably got their hopes up when they saw us create a network that connected everyone on the planet. Big news! A huge evolutionary leap! But twenty years later, having seen how we are using this marvelous technological breakthrough, they are ready to write us off: *PewDiePie? Alex Jones? Okay, shut down the satellite dish.*

SMART MACHINES THAT MAKE STUPID HUMANS

Twenty years ago, many of us believed, naively, that the internet would usher in an age of utopian prosperity: "Picture 20 more years of full employment . . . and improving living standards," the founder of *Wired* predicted in 1999. But then a handful of giant companies monopolized the internet and weaponized the technology against us. We have experienced more dramatic technological change in the past twenty years than in the previous century, and our brains cannot evolve fast enough to keep up. We have been overmatched and overwhelmed by machines.

Though it remains mostly invisible to us, we are surrounded by digital intelligence that vastly outstrips our human intelligence. TikTok is a moronic app full of morons doing moronic things that turn other people into morons. But that moronic app is powered by an intelligence of almost unfathomable sophistication. TikTok's AI-powered code induces addiction so effectively that Facebook, Instagram, Snapchat, and Twitter are desperately racing to reverse-engineer it.

In the past decade, AI has snuck up on us and now powers everything from stock markets to supermarkets, from shipping to shopping. We are hired by machines and fired by machines. We are monitored, measured, and managed by algorithms. Hollywood studios use AI to figure out which movies to green-light. Advertisers use AI tools to find out what to put into their online ads to make them more effective: Puppies do better than kittens. Pictures of doctors and bicycles generate higher engagement. The recommendations you get on Netflix, Amazon, and Spotify and the ads you see on Facebook are chosen by AI algorithms that gather thousands of bits of data about you and sift through it in milliseconds to figure out which words and pictures will prompt your little monkey brain to press the Buy button. At first, we used computers. Now computers use us.

We are being subjected to pressures and stressors unlike anything humans have ever encountered, things we could not have dreamed of a generation ago. Can you imagine how appalled and depressed your Year 2000 self would be if they could see what you look like now? As a former Facebook executive testified to Congress, the algorithms used by Facebook and others "have literally rewired our brains."

LESS HUMAN THAN HUMAN

It's not just that technology has changed; *we* have changed. Our brains buzz with static. We can't focus, can't remember, can't learn, can't think straight. We're doomscrolling, rage tweeting, binge-watching, shitposting, livestreaming. We're *phubbing*—that is, snubbing the people sitting across from us by looking at our phone instead of talking to them. Instead of watching our kids playing soccer or singing off-key in their school play, we hold up our phones and record them. The average person takes more than 450 selfies a year; that's 25,000 in a lifetime. We argue with bots, believing they're people. *We take pictures of our food.*

Seduced and confused by technologies we don't understand, we leap into Ponzi schemes and get fleeced. Crypto investors use real money to buy fake money, then lose almost all of it. NFT buyers have thrown away hundreds of thousands, even millions, of dollars on "bored ape" cartoons *that anyone can copy for free* and that cannot be used for anything other than to remind us that some rich people are also very stupid. In 2021, one wealthy but not very savvy investor paid $2.9 million for a nonfungible token (NFT) of Twitter cofounder Jack Dorsey's first tweet. Months later, when he tried to sell it, he hoped it would fetch $48 million. Instead, the highest bid was $280. Who could have seen that coming?

The internet is making us not just dumb, but angry. That's because, when it comes to creating engagement, anger works. Angry posts get shared more than happy ones. Expressions that connote confusion, anger, fear, and disgust get more views than images of people smiling. So, that's what people make. This bleeds back into our real-world lives. A majority of Americans tell pollsters that they and everyone around them are angrier than in the past. There's so much anger that now we have started getting angry about all the anger. We thought the internet would bring out the best in us. Instead, it has brought out the worst. We thought the internet would bring us together. Instead, it has driven us apart.

Remember when people said things online that they would never say to your face? Now they say those things to your face. Karens are flipping out and demanding to speak to the manager. Hillbillies brawl in buffet restaurants. Conspiracy theorists invade school board meetings to scream about *muh freedom*. Woke people scream about microaggressions; microaggressors scream about wokesters. What used to be called road rage is now everywhere rage. Flight attendants are getting punched in the mouth. The Federal Aviation Administration investigated more than a thousand unruly passenger incidents in 2021, five times as many as in any previous year. Murder rates have soared in some American cities.

Maybe it's entertaining to watch Karens and Kens blowing a gasket in Walmart, or to see QAnon adherents gathering in Dealey Plaza to await the arrival of JFK Jr., but it's not so much fun when an army of whack jobs attacks the US Capitol hoping to lynch the vice president, nor when a not-insignificant number of Americans believe the 2020 election was stolen by space aliens hacking ballot-counting machines with laser cannons on Mars, nor when hundreds of thousands of people die unnecessarily because other people won't get vaccinated, having been convinced that the vaccines are more dangerous than Covid-19 itself and contain tracking devices created by Bill Gates.

The crazy making begins in part by the fact that we become different persons when we go online. Even when we use our real names and believe we are the same person, we're not. Online You is a different person from Real-World You. And many of us have multiple online personas, shape-shifting as we move from one platform or environment to another, creating a new identity with each one. We are turned into performers, playing a cast of characters, strutting and fretting our hours upon the digital stages provided by Discord, Facebook, Instagram, TikTok, and Twitter, signifying mostly nothing.

Social media leads us to develop a mild form of dissociative identity disorder, the condition that used to be called having a split personality and that was the stuff of scary movies like *Psycho* and *Sybil*. A German woman developed this disorder after spending two years playing various roles in online games. The heaviest internet users, internet addicts, often display dissociative symptoms, psychiatrists have found. We're experiencing mental illness at societal scale, driven by a torrent of information. The whole world needs to SITFO.

THE CORTISOL CRISIS

Cortisol and adrenaline are stress hormones associated with the fight-or-flight response, the automatic physiological reaction that saves you from threats, like getting mauled by a tiger or jumped by a mugger. When these hormones are released into the bloodstream, they shut down everything not related to survival and cause your blood pressure, heart rate, and blood sugar to spike.

In short bursts, cortisol and adrenaline help us. We could not survive without them. But chronic exposure wreaks havoc. Being online, especially on your phone, creates a mild but persistent form of stress that causes your body to produce cortisol all the time. Using your phone makes you stressed, but so does *not* using your phone—because when you're not using it, you're wondering if you should check it to see if anything has happened since the last time you looked at it.

Then, when you do grab your phone, you discover that your pain-in-the-ass boss has found a new way to be a pain in the ass and that, meanwhile, on Twitter, someone you don't know wants you to know that you should go kill yourself. Wham! The cortisol floodgates open. You're not getting agitated as heavily as you would if a tiger leapt out of the bushes, but a low-grade dose of cortisol delivered persistently turns out to be worse for you than a huge but short-lived spike. Living with chronically elevated cortisol levels leads to bad things: obesity, type 2 diabetes, heart attacks, Alzheimer's disease. Cortisol creates anxiety and depression. Want to take a guess why antidepressant use and suicide rates have been soaring over the past twenty years?

"Long-term exposure to large doses of cortisol will kill you . . . but slowly," endocrinologist Robert Lustig explains in *The Hacking of the American Mind: The Science Behind the Corporate Takeover of Our Bodies and Brains*. Cortisol causes "poorer cognitive functioning" and interferes with the part of your brain that handles self-control and decision-making, the lobe that "keeps us from doing stupid things," Lustig told the *New York Times*.

Cortisol can cause physical brain damage—docs can see the changes on an MRI. It wrecks your memory and makes it difficult to maintain focus. "Your IQ plummets. Your creativity, your sense of humor—all of that disappears.

You're stupid," psychiatrist Edward Hallowell, author of *Driven to Distraction* and *CrazyBusy*, told *Wired*. Then, you find yourself sprawled on the couch watching zits being popped.

TURN OFF, TUNE OUT

Netflix isn't going to make fewer movies. Facebook, Google, and Twitter won't rein themselves in. Regulators impose fines, but that does nothing. Members of Congress barely understand even the most basic things about the internet, like how tech giants make money. "Senator, we run ads," Zuckerberg once had to explain to Utah senator Orrin Hatch, as if speaking to a child. People who don't know the difference between Twitter and TikTok cannot be relied upon to create laws to control AI algorithms.

So, it's up to us. We can't change the world, but we can protect ourselves from it. At an individual level, this is about guarding our sanity. At a collective level, it is about saving civilization. There are signs, albeit small, that some people may be heeding this advice. In 2022, Facebook started losing subscribers and reported its first-ever revenue decline. In the first half of 2022, Netflix lost subscribers for the first time in its history.

No one is going to quit using the internet or cancel all their streaming subscriptions, nor should they, because, in countless ways, the internet has made our lives immeasurably better, and Netflix and other streaming services produce some great shows. But we can train ourselves and others to consume less content and to use the internet in ways that are less harmful—to apply the brakes on the Anxiety Wheel and SITFO.

Media studies professor Ian Bogost proposes limiting the number of people with whom we connect online. He cites the work of British psychologist Robin Dunbar, who posited that there is a biological limit to the number of people with whom we can have a meaningful connection: about 150. As for really intimate connections, we max out at 15. And there's an inverse relationship between quantity and quality: the more connections you make, the worse those connections are.

Bogost claims that Dunbar's number applies on the internet just as it does in real life. Before the internet, most of us talked less and to fewer people. But the internet enables us to operate at "megascale," making thousands or even millions of shallow connections. Because of this, we have become unmoored from reality and are headed for disaster. "Living amid the ever-rising waste spewed by megascale is unsustainable," Bogost wrote in the *Atlantic* in 2022, in an article headlined "People Aren't Meant to Talk This Much."

Bogost's argument boils down to the notion that everyone needs to STFU: "It's long past time to question a fundamental premise of online life: What if people *shouldn't* be able to say so much, and to so many, so often? . . . Wouldn't it just be better if fewer people posted less stuff, less frequently, and if smaller audiences saw it?"

It would be better. But how to accomplish it? Bogost suggests that internet companies redesign online spaces to limit the number of people we can reach. That's a nice thought, but having done a bit of work inside a social media company, I can assure you that this will never happen. No one I worked with, not a single person, would entertain the idea of restricting users. Every conversation was about getting more people onto the platform and keeping them there longer, stealing them away from other platforms.

The goal is growth. Always growth. Growth at all costs. Social media companies do not employ thousands of moderators to hunt down and scrub away heinous content because they care about safety. They do it because offensive content drives people away. They're not protecting you; they're protecting their business.

HOW TO SITFO

Our phones are FOMO devices, a way to make sure we never miss out on anything. It's significant that the first word in the acronym FOMO is *fear*. We clutch our phones like security blankets, hoping they will soothe us, when ironically they do the exact opposite. They are agitation devices, little battery-powered fear machines.

It's also significant that the word *FOMO* didn't even exist before we had smartphones. In the pre-smartphone era, we missed out on stuff all the time. This didn't scare us. When we felt sad, afraid, or anxious, we bought things: shoes, cars, boats, more shoes, houses. Pick your poison. Consumer culture is driven by the belief that if we just buy enough things, we can fill some empty existential void inside ourselves. Of course, nothing ever fills that yawning pit of despair and neediness. But instead of giving up, we keep going back for more retail therapy.

Now we try to soothe anxiety by consuming not just pointless, trashy things but also pointless, trashy information. We stuff ourselves with as much as we can, three things at once, at double speed, until our brains leak. Noise distracts us and helps us avoid confronting things that scare us half to death—like death. Worried about work? Depressed about a breakup? Feeling bored, anxious, restless, nervous? Tune out and watch TikTok.

Ironically, a lot of people turn to TikTok to get help with their mental health—even as it wrecks their mental health. Just like splurging on shoes or cars, gorging on information doesn't fix your problems; it just makes them worse. The Anxiety Wheel rolls on.

Everyone wants to be happy. Yet we behave in ways that are guaranteed to make us unhappy. We talk about the internet and information overload as if we're helpless against them, as if they were something happening *to* us rather than a choice we are making. But consumption is a choice, and we can stop making it.

The internet is never going to become a quiet place, no more than football stadiums or Midtown Manhattan will. The noise will never go away. But we can. For the sake of our physical health and psychological well-being, we must.

3

STFU ON SOCIAL MEDIA

I quit Facebook first, because that was where I wasted the most time and derived the least benefit. Instead of going cold turkey, I began by removing the Facebook and Messenger apps from my phone. If I wanted to look at Facebook, I would have to use a browser on my computer, which made it harder to jump in and start mindlessly scrolling and commenting. For one week, I felt cravings. After that, the app exerted zero pull. I have not closed down my account. Every few months, I take a peek to see if anyone has messaged me. But that's it. I never post anything. Ever.

Next came Instagram, which was an easy quit, and TikTok, which required some willpower, because TikTok is basically fentanyl on a phone. With these I just deleted the apps from my phone and relied on willpower to get through the first week of withdrawal, after which, as with Facebook, the craving went away.

I kept my LinkedIn account, because it helps me do my work. I stayed on Twitter, because it's a good news filter, but I went into read-only mode, forcing myself to STFU and never tweet, like, or share. One interesting thing I noticed is that Twitter becomes a lot less compelling when you're not talking and can't use it to feed your narcissistic desire to put on a show. This says something about me but also about the app and what it is designed to do—and about the people who do most of the tweeting.

Freed from a prison of my own creation, I began rolling my Anxiety Wheel backward, turning a vicious circle into a virtuous one. For years, I had done as much overtalking online as in real life, and maybe more. I posted photos on Facebook and commented on everything my friends wrote. I dipped into Twitter a dozen times a day and rarely left without tweeting something, or at least commenting and retweeting. I wrote tweet threads. I joined virtual mobs. I dogpiled and got dogpiled. I made fun of dumb politicians. I traded insults.

Stepping away from all that let me claw back hours that I had been wasting on bullshit every day, but more important was the sense of relief I experienced. Overtweeting is the first cousin of overtalking, and it's just as harmful. For years, I felt driven by some pressure to wake up every day and have something clever, witty, or insightful to say. But now that pressure had evaporated, and oddly enough, I had no idea why I had ever felt that compulsion in the first place. The world was not sitting with bated breath, waiting to hear what I would say. The universe did not need or want my thoughts and opinions. Nobody cared when I stopped tweeting. Nobody even noticed. To be sure, my ego felt a bit bruised by this. But that was a small price to pay for how good the rest of me felt. The effect of stepping away from social media is not subtle; it is profound.

Some of the other exercises I've devised in my Five Ways to STFU you can take or leave. Don't like meditation? Fine. You can skip it. But stepping back from social media is not optional. It's mandatory. You do not have to quit altogether, but you must cut way back.

Apply the same rules you follow when speaking. Be disciplined. Be careful. Communicate with intention. Have a plan. Listen more than you speak. Stop talking out of habit, saying things for the sake of saying something. It's difficult enough to do this in ordinary speech, but it's even harder online, because you're going up against tech companies that are determined to get you overtalking and keep you overtalking—to turn you into a tweetaholic.

If you can't curb your social media usage, you will never be able to STFU.

CAN'T STOP, WON'T STOP

One day in 2013, a computer scientist at Google named Tristan Harris had an epiphany: His company was doing bad things to the world. So were Facebook, Instagram, and other social media companies. Social apps had the potential to hurt people, especially kids. Computer scientists were using psychological techniques that had the potential to make people addicted to their apps. Basically, a bunch of young white tech bros, many of them Stanford grads like Harris, were experimenting on human beings, often with calamitous results.

Harris pulled a Jerry Maguire: he sent out a 141-slide presentation criticizing his own company and urging his Google colleagues to redesign products to make them less addictive, less distracting, and, in Google terminology, less evil. The deck went viral inside Google. People loved it. Harris went from being an obscure nobody to a celebrity. Even Larry Page, Google's cofounder and CEO, heard about him.

Google promoted Harris to a new role as a "design ethicist" and seemed to have taken his message to heart. But Harris was hopelessly naive. Google was never going to make its products less addictive. Its business model depended on their becoming *more* addictive. The more time people spent using Google products, the more money Google made.

Finally, Harris left Google and created a nonprofit organization, the Center for Humane Technology, to crusade against the social media industry, which he claimed was "downgrading humans." He gave speeches and even testified before Congress. In 2020, he starred in a Netflix documentary, *The Social Dilemma*, a polemic against social media in which a handful of former execs at Facebook, YouTube, Pinterest, and Twitter repent for their sins. Released during the early days of the binge-watching, social media–obsessed pandemic lockdown, *The Social Dilemma* was viewed 38 million times in its first month, becoming one of Netflix's most-watched documentaries. Finally, Harris had succeeded in getting his message to the world. Everyone was talking about the dangers of social media.

And then: nothing happened.

TikTok gained half a billion more users. Facebook, Instagram, and Snapchat added a combined 400 million. By early 2022, the world was spending 10 billion hours—that's the equivalent of 1.2 million years—on social media every day.

Nobody wants to quit social media, even when they know it's bad for them and will make them feel worse after they use it. That's how addictive this stuff is. One study found that people regret 40 percent of their social media sessions, regarding them as a waste of time, and 60 percent of the time they regret at least part of a social media session. And yet we keep going back. Karl Marx said religion was the "opiate of the masses." Today it's TikTok and Instagram.

"Cigarettes are out. Social media is in. It's the drug of the twenty-first century," British author Simon Sinek once declared. In fact, social media has been found to be even more addictive than cigarettes. And social media companies have become akin to Big Tobacco—peddling a harmful product, targeting kids, and covering up scientific research that might undermine their business.

Companies like Facebook intentionally put you into an agitation loop and turn you into an overtalker. Their business model depends on it. They make money by selling ads, and the more ads they can show you, the more money they make. This means they need to keep you on their site for as long as possible. They use techniques developed nearly a century ago by B. F. Skinner, a psychologist who discovered that if he gave lab rats intermittent rewards, they would try even harder to get them.

It wasn't much of a leap to realize the same trick works on humans. Casinos do this with slot machines. You don't win every time, but once in a while, the bells ring and the lights flash, and so you keep coming back for your treat, and soon your credit card is maxed out and you're cashing in your kid's college fund so you can keep playing. Video games use pings and dings and bright-colored imagery to do the same thing; they call it *juice*.

Computer science programs teach students how to encode addictive techniques into software and create user interfaces that keep people glued to an app. Big social media companies have turbocharged this with artificial intelligence software algorithms that gather trillions of data points about users and hook those data points to supercomputers that can sift them in milliseconds.

Meta, Facebook's parent company, is building the most powerful supercomputer in the world. The company operates eighteen data centers that occupy forty million square feet. Imagine two hundred Walmarts stacked floor to ceiling with racks of computers. This multibillion-dollar digital brain tracks everything you do: every scroll and keystroke; every like, comment, and share; every time you pause to look at an image or read comments under a post; and for how many seconds or milliseconds you stop. TikTok runs an AI system that is even more effective than Facebook's. Their goal is to keep you from leaving, or at least to keep you coming back. That's why everything is scored—how many likes, shares, followers—and why apps ping you with notifications. Sometimes you pick up your phone and find nothing. But sometimes you find a notification. This intermittent reward keeps you coming back, just like those rats in the Skinner box searching for treats. One survey found that people checked their phones 344 times a day—once every four minutes.

ANGER MISMANAGEMENT

The best way to keep you engaged with the app is to get you talking—not just reading your feed but posting, tweeting, sharing, liking, commenting. And the best way to get you talking is to make you angry. The digital brain figures out what kind of content pushes your buttons, and it steers that into your feed. Social media companies moderate content and filter out a lot of horrible stuff. But some bad content—hate speech, conspiracy theories, misinformation—drives engagement. "That stuff is the lubricant of the business," says Roger McNamee, who was an early investor in Facebook but later became a critic of the company after coming to believe it was dangerous. The artificial intelligence systems powering social apps "know how you behave under stress. They find out what you are like when nobody is looking. That's a total payday for these guys," McNamee told me.

Users who care about boosting their numbers quickly figure out that when they post angry or emotionally charged comments, they get more treats—shares, comments, likes—so they start doing more of that. According to researchers at Yale who sifted 1.2 million tweets by seven thousand Twitter users, users' tweets become angrier and more extreme over time, and their moral outrage grows. "The rewards of social media create positive feedback loops that exacerbate outrage," says Molly Crockett, the neuroscientist who led the Yale study. Most significant, the Yale researchers found that those people also start posting more frequently. They get turned into overtalkers, roaming their virtual worlds looking for arguments.

Online outrage spills back into your real-world life. People who rant online tend to be angrier in their personal lives, researchers have found. The anger you experience online stays with you when you log off.

DOPAMINE AND DEPRESSION

Those little treats and rewards that you get on a social app deliver bursts of dopamine, a feel-good chemical produced in the brain that acts as a neurotransmitter. But dopamine puts you on a roller coaster. Each time your brain produces dopamine, it simultaneously tries to level things out and restore balance by switching off some of your dopamine receptors—offsetting pleasure with pain, according to Stanford psychiatrist Anna Lembke, author of *Dopamine Nation: Finding Balance in the Age of Indulgence.*

As the dopamine wanes, you crash, and you want another hit. So, back you go to Instagram. Eventually, the dopamine doesn't get you high; you need it just to feel normal. If you try to stop, you experience withdrawal symptoms like you would with heroin. So, you keep going back. But also, the cycle sends you spiraling into anxiety and depression, which are leading causes of overtalking.

The more attention you get, the more you crave. There is never enough. Who doesn't want to be catapulted out of their life of quiet desperation and into the spotlight? Even Elon Musk, the richest person in the world, who already lives in the spotlight, wants even more. Addicted to the adulation he gets on Twitter, Musk spends his time shitposting and trolling on the platform, putting on a show for his audience of more than ninety million followers.

The hunger for attention is really a quest for deeper things: connection, validation, acceptance, popularity, a sense of belonging. In a way, we're searching for love—from friends, strangers, and even bots. We may or may not find love, and the love we find may or may not be real, but in our quest for it, we do exactly what the computer scientists on the other side of the screen want us to do: We talk. And talk. And talk some more.

Lembke used to prescribe antidepressants to patients suffering from addiction to social media, but she found she could accomplish the same benefit by prescribing a "dopamine fast," which means taking a break from all screens and shutting off the supply of dopamine for up to a month. Lembke also suggests setting aside one day a week when you don't look at any screens.

Basically, she prescribes a great big dose of STFU.

You can feel the benefits almost immediately. Ask any kid who has gone to a camp or school trip where smartphones are not allowed. "It was amazing. I felt great. I was so much happier" is how my son describes a two-week outing to Costa Rica during which all the kids had to give up their phones and talk to one another. They loved it. They were happy, social, and had a wonderful time. But as soon as they got to the airport to fly home and had their phones returned to them, the camaraderie vanished. Kids who had just spent two weeks building close friendships immediately disappeared back into their cocoons. "Everyone changed. It was like we all became irritable," my son says.

ALONE AGAIN, UNNATURALLY

In addition to anxiety and depression, heavy social media use causes a sense of isolation and loneliness. That's ironic, because social media sites were supposed to bring people together and help us build connections. But social media turns out to be not so social after all. "Alone together" is how MIT sociologist Sherry Turkle describes the phenomenon. We're constantly connected but all by ourselves. Turkle worries that we are destroying our ability to feel empathy and to have genuine conversations, and she recommends that we create "sacred spaces" where we put away phones and have face-to-face conversations. Just having a phone sitting on the table causes people to share less with each other, she says.

Meaningful conversations have been found to be crucial to emotional and physical well-being. But in one survey, nearly half of people said that online talking got in the way of their having deep conversations in real life. According to Emma Walker from LifeSearch, the insurance broker in the United Kingdom that conducted the survey, "This is proving to be a barrier to the traditional 'deep and meaningful,' meaning that we're not getting to the bottom of the issues that matter."

In another survey, 70 percent of women said technology tools stole time from real conversations and interfered with their relationships. A 2021 study found that Instagram had negative effects on romantic partnerships, contributing to "an increase in both conflict and negative outcomes." According to another 2021 survey, nearly 60 percent of people say social media had hurt their relationships with family and friends.

A big part of having meaningful conversations is being able to listen, but "social media has taught us to talk rather than listen," claims Kalev Leetaru, a senior fellow at the George Washington University Center for Cyber and Homeland Security. "Social media has failed to live up to the most important part of its promise: bringing us together. Instead of creating a place where we can all come together and engage in conversation in the global town square, we've ended up with a great gladiator match of megaphones in which the loudest and most toxic one prevails." Social media brings out our inner narcissist: researchers say people talk about themselves 60 percent of the time in real conversation but 80 percent of the time on Facebook and Twitter.

Computer scientist Jaron Lanier, a hardcore antisocialist, argues in his book *Ten Arguments for Deleting Your Social Media Accounts Right Now* that there is no safe way to use social media, and that the only solution is to not use social media at all. But most of us aren't going to quit completely. Nor should we, because we would be giving up the good things about social media, which are significant. On social media, people make new friends, stay in touch, share their stories, and support one another. Some research has found that Instagram harms teenage girls, but other studies have found that more than 80 percent of teens say social media makes them feel more connected to their friends, and nearly 70 percent say people on social media platforms have supported them when they were going through difficult or challenging times.

Social media became a lifeline during the Covid-19 lockdown, a way for people to reduce loneliness and depression by staying in touch when they could not meet in person. For every study that shows social media hurting real-life connections, there are others showing that social media helps people stay connected to family and friends and might even improve relationships and bring people closer. This mix of good and bad makes it even more difficult to strike the right balance and figure out when to STFU.

REGRETS, I'VE HAD A FEW

In June 2022, journalists at the *Washington Post* beclowned themselves and their publication by creating a mess on Twitter. David Weigel, a reporter, retweeted a sexist joke, then deleted it and apologized. That was not enough, said his colleague Felicia Sonmez, who demanded the *Post* take action. The paper suspended Weigel. A frenzy ensued, with mobs from both sides unleashed on one another, turning an Anxiety Wheel into an Anxiety Tornado. Things escalated further when a third journalist from the *Post* tweeted that Sonmez should not have rallied the internet against a colleague. The executive editor of the *Post* wrote an email to the staff (which of course was leaked onto Twitter) that said, basically, "You kids stop fighting!" *Post* staffers started tweeting about how much they loved the *Post*. Sonmez carried on criticizing the paper—and got fired. The *Post* looked like an out-of-control kindergarten. The rest of the world sat back like Puck in *A Midsummer Night's Dream*, marveling at what fools these mortals be. "Are There Any Adults at the Washington Post?" one pundit reveled.

There were no winners—except Twitter, which makes money off rage storms. So, here's a thought exercise. Imagine that Twitter did not exist and that these people had to work this out among themselves, in private. Wouldn't all of them, and all of us, have been better off? As Sonmez discovered, the problem with Twitter is that you're always just 280 characters away from losing your job. Spend enough time in the Twittersphere and eventually you will tweet your way into trouble. More than half of Americans say they have posted something on social media they later regretted, and

16 percent (one in six) say they regret a post at least once a week, a YouGov America survey found.

"I Regretted the Minute I Pressed Share" was the title of a 2011 study by researchers at Carnegie Mellon University who turned up amazing stories of people wrecking their lives on Facebook, sometimes because they posted in anger but also just by accident, including a woman who uploaded a video of her baby's first steps but accidentally also uploaded a video of herself having sex with her husband. She did not realize her mistake until the next day, when she found comments from her friends and family, and her husband's coworkers. A study at New York University Grossman School of Medicine found that more than a third of young people have posted something on social media while they were high, and 20 percent say they posted something they later regretted.

Stoned posting is similar to drunk-dialing, researchers said, but the difference is that instead of embarrassing yourself to one person, you're making a fool out of yourself in front of the whole world, and unlike phone calls, the internet is forever. That photo of you snorting a line of coke, or puking outside a bar, might show up years later when you're applying for a job.

Peter Sagal, host of the *Wait Wait . . . Don't Tell Me!* game show on National Public Radio, once published a list of rules for Twitter, the first of which is "You will and have regretted many tweets. You will never regret not tweeting."

Ironically, he wrote this on Twitter. Still, it's good advice.

WAYS TO CUT BACK ON SOCIAL MEDIA

The best way to stay off social media is to keep busy doing something else, says Cal Newport, a computer science professor at Georgetown University and author of *Digital Minimalism: Choosing a Focused Life in a Noisy World*. Making resolutions and relying on willpower will not do the trick, Newport says. Instead, he recommends a one-month "digital detox," during which you forgo all digital technology you do not absolutely need. After that, you can go back, but do it slowly, in increments, small doses—becoming a "digital minimalist."

As for being productive, Newport is a man of his word. He has published eight books, the first three of which he wrote on the side while completing his PhD from MIT. The thirty-nine-year-old Newport is a full-time tenured professor who teaches undergraduate and graduate courses at Georgetown while also doing research and publishing academic papers. He also has recorded 198 podcast episodes and in his spare time does some public speaking.

He does not have a social media account.

You might not be ready to handle a one-month digital detox, but there are other ways to become a digital minimalist. Here are some clever ways to limit your social media use:

Conduct an inventory. Chances are you are spending a lot more time on social media than you think. Your phone can track your usage and give you a daily or weekly report. How many social media apps do you use? How many hours a week do you spend on each one? Which ones do you use the most? Which one do you find the most addictive? Which one do you find the least useful? Such an inventory will help you make a game plan. And seeing how much time you're wasting might prompt you to take action.

Delete apps from your phone. Force yourself to use social media only via a browser on your computer. That way you can't just grab your phone and start snacking on social out of habit.

Uninstall and reinstall. Nimesh Patel, a comedian and former *Saturday Night Live* writer, limits his Instagram use by uploading and then deleting the app each time he uses it: "I check it in the morning, and then I delete it. Then I check it at night and delete it again."

Indulge, but set limits. Arthur C. Brooks, a professor at the Harvard Kennedy School, recommends scheduling a certain amount of time every day to do nothing but use social media. But don't let yourself use it at any other time. The key when using social media is to engage in "mindful scrolling," which means fully concentrating on what you're doing, being "all about the phone for those minutes, as if it were your job," Brooks advises.

Schedule a weekly "digital Sabbath." Choose one day a week when you avoid social media. If possible, don't use your phone or other electronic devices at all.

"Lose" your phone. Location matters. Put the phone in a different room and turn off the ringer. Just keep it out of reach. Same thing at bedtime. Do not keep your phone on the bedside table. At the very least, keep it on the other side of the room.

Fight apps with apps. If you can't gin up the willpower to control your usage—and most of us cannot—get one of the many anti-distraction apps that block you from using an app for a certain period of time. One of the most popular is Freedom, which works on computers and smartphones, costs forty dollars a year, and has a loyal following among employees at Apple, Google, and Microsoft and researchers at Harvard, MIT, and Stanford. Another, called One Sec, adds a delay that makes it take longer for a social app to load, and then asks if you still want to open the app. The creator says One Sec broke his addiction and made him more productive, but it also relieved the anxiety and depression that had been building. "In the end, this is about mental health," he told me.

Buy a dumb phone. This is a pretty brute-force approach, but you can try replacing your smartphone with one that won't run apps. You might buy it as a second phone and carry it with you part of the time, which gives you a break from apps.

Use a smartwatch instead of your smartphone. Same concept as getting a dumb phone: buy an Apple Watch (or something like it) that has cellular capability and use it as your phone. There are versions of social apps that run on smartwatches, but the experience is awful enough that you won't be drawn to them.

Turn off notifications. Those little pings and buzzes and words popping up on your screen are designed to distract you and drag you back into the app. Unless your job requires you to be constantly on standby for an important client, or for some other reason you cannot be disconnected from an app, turn off these notifications.

Go gray. Change the display on your phone to grayscale, which wipes away all the color, turning your phone and every app on it into an old black-and-white TV. Our brains crave shiny objects and bright colors. That's why app developers use them. Interface designers test thousands of colors and combinations to learn which ones are most addictive. Grayscale renders their work futile.

Shift into read-only mode. Force yourself to stop

posting, tweeting, sharing, or liking. This requires some discipline, but you will be surprised by how much less compelling an app becomes when you're not participating.

Try the W.A.I.T. method. Before putting thumb to keyboard, ask yourself, *Why am I tweeting?* Do you have some special, unique knowledge that will inform the debate on a subject being discussed on Twitter? Are you asking a question, genuinely looking for information, and hoping to learn something? What are you hoping to accomplish? What's in it for you? It has been my experience that whenever I ask myself *Why am I tweeting?* I almost never have a good answer. And the more often I STFU on social media, the easier it becomes for me to STFU during the rest of my life.

4

MANSPLAINING, MANTERRUPTING, AND MANALOGUES

Men are the champions of overtalking—and talking over. We bulldoze. We hog the floor. We mansplain, manterrupt, and deliver manalogues. In my house, they're called Danalogues, and part of my STFU practice has been to stop engaging in them.

Men are especially obnoxious in the workplace, even to the most accomplished and powerful women in the world, including Supreme Court justices and the chief technology officer of the United States. I once watched my wife get bullied by a guy during the Q&A period after she presented a conference paper. He talked over her, interrupted her, wouldn't let her speak, and practically shouted at her. Afterward, when I told her how outraged I was, she said, "Don't you know? This happens to women all the time."

Most men aren't usually as openly hostile as the guy who badgered my wife. But men talk over women all the time and often do not even realize they're doing it. One study found that women at work get mansplained up to six times a week, more than three hundred times a year.

Nearly two-thirds of women believe men don't even know when they're mansplaining. And two out of five women say men have told them that they, the *women*, come on too strong!

Men overtalk so constantly and regularly that it has become normalized. In fact, it's rare for it not to happen. Next time you're in a group of men and women, sit back and watch. Count the interruptions. See who does the interrupting and who gets interrupted. Take note of how often a man lays claim to expertise that he does not possess or delivers a confident lecture about something he just read about in the *New York Times* or the *Atlantic* as if the ideas are his own. Once you see it, you can't unsee it.

You can, however, unlearn it. And doing that will pay off. If you are a man and you want to be a better partner and a better parent, if you want to be a great colleague and advance your career, if you want to stand out from all the other men, apply the Five Ways to STFU. If you're a woman, or a girl, author Soraya Chemaly recommends that you practice saying the following three sentences every day: "Stop interrupting me." "I just said that." "No explanation needed."

THE MYTH OF THE OVERTALKING WOMAN

What's weird is that while men are by far more likely to be overtalkers, women historically have been portrayed as chatterboxes and gossips, stuck with the stereotype that they talk more than men. In 2006, neuropsychiatrist Louann Brizendine seemed to confirm the stereotype when she claimed, in her bestseller *The Female Brain*, that women speak twenty thousand words a day while men speak only seven thousand. Apparently, she got the numbers from *Why Men Don't Listen and Women Can't Read Maps*, a self-help book written by Allan Pease, a bestselling author and body language expert. But (a) Pease was counting "communication events" like facial expressions and gestures, not spoken words; and (b) it's unclear where he got his numbers. Brizendine's claim struck some experts as ridiculous—think about it: *three times as much?*—but the media loved it. The old stereotype was true! Science says so!

When an interviewer asked Brizendine whether she was just rehashing an outdated trope, she replied, "A stereotype always has an aspect of truth to it, or it wouldn't be a stereotype. I am talking about the biological basis behind behaviors that we all know about."

But her numbers were wrong. When researchers at the University of Texas at Austin created an experiment to check Brizendine's claim, they found that women and men both averaged out to about sixteen thousand words a day—and the three most extreme overtalkers in the study were men. Brizendine had made an honest mistake, and to her credit, she acknowledged that mistake and removed those numbers from later editions of her book. But those numbers have been used in hundreds of articles, and the internet is forever. There are certainly people who still believe them and cite them.

Brizendine's flub raised an interesting question. Why did the numbers resonate so deeply? Why did they stir up such emotions and evoke such a strong reaction—from both men and women alike? It's an example of the Big Lie theory: say something enough times, over a long enough period of time, and people believe it.

The stereotype cuts across cultures. "Women's tongues are like lamb's tails; they are never still" is an old English saying. In Japan, they say, "Where there are women and geese, there is noise." The Chinese say, "The tongue is the sword of a woman, and she never lets it become rusty." Shakespeare's plays are filled with depictions of women as shrews and fishwives. The phrase "old wives' tales" originally referred to the lies or immoral stories told by women. The word *gossip* comes from the Old English *godsibb*, which originally meant "godparent" but, by the 1500s, had evolved to mean "slanderous talk and rumors spread by women." Go back even further, and you'll find Saint Paul describing widows as "idlers, gadding about from house to house, and not only idlers but gossips and busybodies, saying what they should not."

In the Middle Ages, women were convicted of "sins of the tongue" and punished by being paraded around the town square, dunked into a river, or forced to wear a "scold's bridle," an iron cage that went over the head with a bridle that pushed down the tongue, making it impossible for the wearer to speak. In the United Kingdom, the scold's bridle remained in use into the early 1900s.

Some men still cling to the belief that women talk more than men. In 2021, Yoshiro Mori, the eighty-three-year-old head of the Tokyo Olympic Games organizing committee and former prime minister, responded to a suggestion that the committee include more women members by saying the meetings would drag on too long because women talk too much. In 2017, David Bonderman, a seventy-five-year-old private equity investor and member of the Uber board of directors, declared that adding more women to the board would mean "it's much more likely to be more talking."

The truth, of course, is exactly the opposite: in most situations, especially professional ones, men do way more of the talking.

MANTERRUPTIONS

In 2014, Kieran Snyder, an executive at a tech company, ran an experiment. Over the course of fifteen hours of meetings, she logged every time someone interrupted. Snyder, who has a PhD in linguistics, counted 314 interruptions, and two-thirds of them were made by men—meaning men interrupted twice as often as women. More interesting, when men interrupted, 70 percent of the time they interrupted a woman. The imbalance was made even more dramatic by the fact that women comprised only 40 percent of the group. Also, when women did the interrupting, they were far likelier (89 percent of the time) to interrupt other women than to interrupt men. Snyder's conclusion: "Whenever women take a speaking turn, they are getting interrupted," she wrote in *Slate*. No woman she knew was surprised by what she found. "Women in tech have mostly responded, 'Yeah, duh,'" she wrote.

Snyder's suggested solution was not for men to STFU, but for women to become more aggressive about interrupting and, especially, to learn to interrupt men. "How to Get Ahead as a Woman in Tech: Interrupt Men" was the headline on her article. "The results suggest that women don't advance in their careers beyond a certain point without learning to interrupt, at least in this male-dominated tech setting," she concluded.

According to a 2020 study by Dartmouth sociologist Janice McCabe, male college students speak 1.6 times as much as women. They are more likely to speak without raising their hands, to interrupt, and to hold forth for longer amounts of time. The male-female imbalance is even more pronounced among professors and graduate students at academic colloquiums, where men speak twice as much as women, according to a 2017 study by researchers at Rice University. In elementary school, boys talk three times as much as girls, but teachers perceive girls as more talkative. When asked how they perceived the balance of speaking in a discussion, men considered things were equal when women spoke only 15 percent of the time, and when women spoke 30 percent of the time, the men considered the discussion to be dominated by women, according to Australian feminist scholar Dale Spender. A male science teacher who established a near-equal balance of girls and boys talking perceived that girls were doing 90 percent of the talking. Spender's famous quote: "The talkativeness of women has been gauged in comparison not with men but with silence. Women have not been judged on the grounds of whether they talk more than men, but of whether they talk more than silent women."

A Stanford study compared two-part conversations between two men, between two women, and between a man and a woman. In the same-sex conversations, there were seven interruptions. In the man-woman conversation, there were forty-eight interruptions, and forty-six of them were by the man. Researchers at George Washington University found that men interrupted women 33 percent more often than they interrupted men. Professors at the Northwestern Pritzker School of Law studied US Supreme Court transcripts and found that women justices were three times more likely to be interrupted than their male counterparts and far less likely to interrupt others. Only 4 percent of interruptions were by women, while 66 percent of interruptions were aimed at them.

In the first Obama administration, women staffers were outnumbered by men two to one and found that their ideas and suggestions frequently would be ignored during meetings, but then a few weeks later their male colleagues would present the same ideas and claim them as their own. The women staffers fought back by devising a strategy they called "amplification." When one woman made a point, other women would repeat that point while giving credit to her. This made it harder for men to steal ideas and take credit for them. Eventually, the president noticed what they were doing and started calling on women more often during meetings.

WHY WE MANSPLAIN

One problem, according to Deborah Tannen, a linguistics professor at Georgetown University, is that men are socialized to behave this way and may not even be aware that they're doing it. Men are trained to assert themselves and to pursue power and dominance through speech. They speak to achieve status, and women speak to achieve connection— which sounds like another stereotype, at least as it relates to women, but the claim about men rings true, researchers say. Mansplaining serves the same purpose as manspreading: asserting dominance by occupying more space.

This begins in childhood, when boys focus on status and quickly establish pecking orders in groups, struggling to get a "one-up" position, while girls try to build rapport, Tannen says. As adults, men use speech to demonstrate skill or knowledge. In the workplace, men use "I" in situations where women use "we." "Women are less likely than men to have learned how to blow their own horn," Tannen wrote in *Harvard Business Review*.

In one experiment, incoming college students were asked to predict what grades they would get in the year ahead. When women wrote down their answers and put them in an envelope, they predicted higher grades than when they were asked to declare their predictions in public to the researchers. Men predicted the same grades in both situations—they had no qualms about appearing overconfident.

The stereotype about men not wanting to stop and ask for directions is based in truth; men see asking questions as lowering their status. The same goes for the workplace, where men fear losing by appearing to be ignorant, Tannen says. John Gray, author of *Men Are from Mars, Women Are from Venus*, analyzed interviews with one hundred thousand executives to discover that 80 percent of women say they will ask questions even when they know the answer and that 72 percent of men say that women ask too many questions. Good grief!

When men hear a complaint, they believe they have been given a challenge and are expected to offer advice or devise a solution. So, they end up mansplaining. Men also are more prone to interrupt or to challenge others in conversation, says Rob Kendall, an author and consultant who studies conversation styles.

Eric Schmidt, the former chairman of Google, participated in a panel discussion at a conference and constantly interrupted the only woman, who was Megan Smith, the chief technology officer of the United States and a former top Google executive. Schmidt seemed to have no idea that he was doing this until, during the Q&A period, the woman who ran Google's Global Diversity and Talent Program pointed it out as an example of unconscious bias toward women.

Manterrupting is gender bias playing itself out in speech. It's men believing that they are more important than women and deserving of higher status. It's Ego Talkers believing that their opinions are better and, so, deserve more time. *It's not that you're not smart, Megan Smith. It's just that I'm so much smarter.*

Mansplaining has little to do with who you are as an individual and mostly to do with your gender. Trans men and women have a unique opportunity to see this in action, says Jessica Nordell, an author and consultant who studies gender bias in the workplace. Trans men are interrupted less frequently after their transition, Nordell has found, and trans women have the opposite experience.

Ben Barres, a neurobiologist at Stanford University who lived as "Barbara Barres" until transitioning in 1997, described receiving remarkably different treatment as Ben: he was interrupted less frequently and praised more effusively for his work. "People who don't know I am transgendered treat me with much more respect: I can even complete a whole sentence without being interrupted by a man," wrote Barres, who died in 2017. Once, when he gave a presentation at a seminar, someone in the audience who did not realize Ben Barres and Barbara Barres were the same person commented, "Ben Barres gave a great seminar today, but then, his work is so much better than his sister's."

Another Stanford scientist, a trans woman named Joan Roughgarden, has had the opposite experience: she says she was taken less seriously and treated with less respect after transitioning. Roughgarden, an evolutionary biologist, has described being interrupted, shouted at, and even physically intimidated by male scientists who did not agree with her ideas. Her salary drifted down. Comparing her situation to that of Ben Barres, Roughgarden said, "Ben has migrated into the center, whereas I have had to migrate into the periphery."

ALL IS NOT LOST

Men need to change—and according to one expert, most of us want to do it, if someone can just show us how. It begins with recognizing that men have a propensity to interrupt and talk over people, especially women. We might not even know we're doing it. And we get away with overtalking and interrupting "because society has accepted that it's normal and natural that men tend to talk more," according to Joanna Wolfe, a professor at Carnegie Mellon University who uses undergraduate engineering students as her test subjects to research the way men and women communicate with each other.

Wolfe told me about what she calls "positive future focus," a strategy that enables women to assert themselves without suffering a social penalty. Instead of expressing anger or negative feelings, you should focus on positive outcomes, saying things like "We can make this meeting a lot more efficient if we give everyone a chance to speak without being interrupted." In the case of airing a grievance, Wolfe found the most effective course of action is to focus on the future rather than the past and on facts rather than emotions.

One bright spot, Wolfe discovered, is that once they see how much they interrupt and talk over women, some men will work on their communication skills. In one experiment, Wolfe and her colleagues videotaped small teams of engineering students having meetings and then showed the recordings to each person. In one group, there were two men and one woman, and when one of the men watched the recording, he was taken aback to see how he and the other man talked over, interrupted, and ignored their female colleague. "He said, 'Oh my God. I can't believe myself. I can't believe how rude we were,'" Wolfe told me. "He was shocked. He saw how excluded the woman was. He saw some of her facial expressions that he had not seen before." He vowed to do better.

HOW TO BREAK YOUR INTERRUPTING HABIT

The goal of STFU is to find ways to communicate more effectively with other people. That means learning how to stop interrupting people, but also learning how to interrupt someone politely if or when interrupting becomes necessary—for example, when you need to shut down an overtalker. To learn how to stop interrupting, some of my Five Ways to STFU work really well. "When possible, say nothing," and "Become an active listener" are obvious choices. Here are two other ways to break the habit of interrupting:

Record and transcribe. Zoom makes this easy. In a one-on-one or group meeting, get permission to record it and then listen to the recording afterward and/or send the audio to a service like Rev to have it transcribed. For me, seeing the words on a page has the most impact. You can measure how much each person talks just by looking at the size of their paragraphs. Just like those male students who participated in Joanna Wolfe's studies at Carnegie Mellon, you may be surprised by how much interrupting you do.

Take notes. A common reason for interrupting is that you've just had a great idea about something the other person said and you worry that if they keep going, you will forget what you want to say. Or the other person will move on to other topics, and the conversation will drift away from the point you want to make. Pro tip: instead of interrupting, keep a pen handy and jot down your idea so that you can come back to it later. Extra pro tip: sometimes when the other person sees you taking a note, they will stop to ask if you have something to say.

WALKING THE TIGHTROPE: DEFENDING AGAINST INTERRUPTERS

Fighting back can be tricky, especially for women. Studies show that when men call someone out for interrupting, they are seen in a positive light, but when women do it, they're seen negatively. As former Facebook chief operating officer Sheryl Sandberg once wrote, "When a woman speaks in a professional setting, she walks a tightrope. Either she's barely heard or she's judged as too aggressive."

There are ways to be assertive without falling from the tightrope. Studies have found that people who speak more directly, use shorter sentences, and look potential interrupters directly in the eye get interrupted less frequently. Word choice matters, too. Say "I know" instead of "I think" or "I believe." Say "will" instead of "might." And start out strong. The Northwestern researchers who studied Supreme Court interruptions found that most interruptions occurred at the beginning of a justice's comments and often when a woman justice began with a polite phrase like "May I ask . . ." Over time, women justices learned to be less polite. You can do the same.

Here are five other tactics:

Stop, wait, continue. Virgin Group founder Richard Branson shares a trick he learned from George Whitesides, the former CEO of Virgin Galactic. If someone interrupted Whitesides, he would stop in midsentence, let the other person finish, and then just keep going where he left off. The technique was a silent scold, an effective way to train people to stop interrupting—"a thing of beauty to watch," Branson writes in *The Virgin Way: Everything I Know About Leadership.*

Anticipate and regulate. If you are running the meeting, set the ground rules before the meeting begins. Or set them before you speak: "This is important, so let me say the whole thing before jumping in." If *that guy*—the serial offender—is in the meeting, look at him directly while you say it.

Call the other person out. "Mr. Vice President, I'm speaking," Kamala Harris famously said when Mike Pence kept interrupting her during a debate. She pointed out what

he was doing and was calm but assertive. She looked like
a leader. You can take a more polite route: "I have a few
more points to make. Can you hold off until I get through
them?" Or this: "I want to hear your feedback, if you'll
hold off until I'm done."

Just keep talking. This one's tricky, but some people
can pull it off. You don't have to talk faster or louder. Just
keep talking. This works best when you are dealing with
that guy, because others will side with you and may consider you a hero for doing what they wish they had the guts
to do.

Talk to the interrupter privately. This might be someone who interrupts you, or it could be a person who has a
habit of interrupting everyone. Shaming him by calling him
out in a meeting might be counterproductive, but a private
talk can be effective. The interrupter may not even know
he's doing it, and he may be grateful that you're pointing
this out. Frame it as an attempt to help him.

HOW TO INTERRUPT POLITELY

Sometimes you need to interrupt, and there are ways to do
this that are not rude. The main thing is to be clear that
you are not hijacking the conversation and that you want
the other person to continue speaking after you make your
comment.

Ask permission. You can do this with a facial expression
or a small gesture that indicates you want to say something.
Or say, "I'm sorry, may I interrupt for a second?" Another
one: "I'm sorry, but what you've just said is important. May
I ask a question before you continue?"

Start with an apology. Every interruption should begin

with "I'm sorry" and should be followed by "I want to hear the rest of what you have to say. I just didn't understand something you said."

MEN: THIS IS ON US

Teaching women how to defend themselves against inter- rupters is great, but in a perfect world, we would not have to do it. The burden falls to men, and like Joanna Wolfe at Carnegie Mellon, I believe many of us want to do bet- ter. Start by being extra vigilant when you're talking with women. Recognize that you probably have a tendency to manterrupt and also that, as soon as you do, the women you're talking to will lower their opinion of you and put less value on what you say.

Be aware of the dynamic and overcompensate for it. Don't just let women finish what they want to say, but also wait a beat before you start speaking. And don't man- splain. Imagine that the conversation is a basketball, and don't be a ball hog. Speak four sentences, max, and then pass the ball.

Consciously or subconsciously, women expect men to manterrupt, mansplain, and deliver manalogues. The men who don't do these things stand out and are seen in a more positive light. They're also more persuasive. Be one of those men.

5

STFU AS MEDICINE

Thirty minutes of moderate exercise per day will keep you healthy and help you live longer. So will taking ten thousand steps a day and getting eight hours of sleep. But changing the way you talk might be just as important. Speaking with intention, listening more, spending time in silence, and—as I'll discuss in this chapter—even changing the words you use can reduce anxiety, depression, and your chances of developing inflammatory diseases. Basically, you can use STFU as medicine.

"Our most prevalent behavior is speech. It's talking to other people. But until relatively recently, we were not studying it," says Matthias Mehl, a social psychologist at the University of Arizona who has been searching for connections between speech and well-being for the past twenty years. "But it's profoundly fascinating, this idea that psychological processing could have positive and negative consequences in the physical body."

Mehl first gained attention when he debunked the numbers in *The Female Brain* that suggested that women speak three times as many words per day as men. He did this by having four hundred college students spend a few days carrying around a device called an Electronically Activated Recorder, or EAR, which turns itself on at random intervals and records what it hears. When Mehl averaged out the numbers, he found that men and women both spoke about sixteen thousand words a day. And the three most talkative test subjects were men.

From there, Mehl started using the EAR to study not just how many words people spoke, but also which words they used. How much time did people spend engaged in meaningful, substantive conversations, and how much of their daily speech was given over to small talk and chitchat? And what, if anything, did that say about them?

In a report called "Eavesdropping on Happiness," Mehl and his team found that people who spent more time having good conversations and less time making small talk were happier than everyone else. They did this by asking test subjects to fill out reports in which they gauged how satisfied they were with their lives, gathering input from people who knew the subjects, and then calculating a "happiness score" for each person and matching it to their conversation data. The happiest person in the study spent only 10 percent of their speaking time on small talk. The unhappiest person spent nearly 30 percent.

The bottom line, Mehl concluded, was that good conversations have such a profound effect on emotional well-being that they "might be a key ingredient to a satisfied life." He believes you can make yourself happier by paying attention to the way you speak and making an effort to have better conversations.

But how do you define a "good" conversation? How do you have one? Basically, you STFU. Good conversations are not necessarily about talking more. In fact, they usually involve talking *less*. "Our data is very consistent with the possibility that the world would be a better place if people in conversations ended up listening more and talking less," Mehl says. "The best way to elicit meaningful conversations is by asking questions."

You don't have to forgo small talk and chitchat altogether, Mehl says. Just try, at least once a day, to have a conversation that goes beyond how nice the weather has been and how quickly this summer is flying by. You don't have to discuss anything as lofty as the meaning of life or the existence of the afterlife. You might have a good talk with your teenager about school or plan a vacation with your partner. Mundane conversations can evolve into deeper discussions of dreams and aspirations.

There's an art to shifting an ordinary conversation into a "good" conversation. Mehl told me about going for a walk and running into his neighbor, who had recently had cancer surgery. "I asked him, 'How are you doing?' And not in the sense of 'Hi, what's up?', but of 'No, really, how are you *doing*?'" And we ended up having a good conversation. That's the beauty of it. The starting point of a good conversation can be not that far away from small talk. It's asking 'How are you?' but in a slightly more genuine and concerned way. And from there, the conversation unfolds."

It's also about being authentic. "The idea is that, in this conversation, can I squeeze in something authentic?" Mehl says. "It's interesting, because what do we mean by 'authentic'? We mean that you're not putting up a disguise. You're allowing a part of yourself to be seen or heard. Which means you're expressing things that are consistent with your values. You get away from the weather and the Super Bowl, and you get to the things that matter, the things that are your core values."

TAKE TWO CONVERSATIONS AND CALL ME IN THE MORNING

If having good conversations can boost your psychological well-being, could it also improve your physical health? It seems kind of crazy, but Mehl suspected there might be something to it.

The idea that speech and health are related—that you can "talk yourself better"—has been kicking around for a long time. Fifty years ago, there was a boom in psychosomatic medicine, the notion that people might be able to use emotional and social behavior to cure or relieve physical ailments—the classic example being the belief that positive thinking can improve your chance of surviving cancer. Many docs say this is complete quackery, though at least one study of cancer patients found that positive thinking contributed to strengthening patients' immune systems and helping them develop more cancer-fighting cells.

In the 1970s, psychologist James J. Lynch discovered that whenever you speak, your blood pressure goes up, and whenever you listen, your blood pressure goes down. He would put on demonstrations in which he called volunteers up onstage, hooked them to a blood pressure monitor, and told them to start speaking. Immediately, and to the delight of the audience, their blood pressure would rise.

People with hypertension were especially sensitive: when they started talking, their blood pressure soared. Overtalkers also had an exaggerated response.

Lynch proposed treating people with hypertension by teaching them to speak in a more relaxed way—basically, using speech as medicine. "How can we enjoy conversation yet keep blood pressure down?" he wondered. "By listening more, by breathing regularly while talking, by alternating between talking and paying attention to what the other person is saying." Again, this was STFU as medicine. And if you're an overtalker, take note: you have an extra-high risk of suffering physical harm from overtalking.

The problem with the work being done back in the 1970s is that the technology available to researchers was Stone Age compared to what exists today. People like Lynch were finding correlations and making educated guesses based on intuition. Mehl, however, had the benefit of using genomics to quantify results when he set out to find connections. Just as with the "Eavesdropping" study, he equipped people with EAR devices and recorded and transcribed what they said, but instead of matching their conversation quality to happiness scores, he matched them to genetic information. He did this with Steve Cole, a psychologist at UCLA who studies the way social environments influence gene expression. They found that people who spent more time having good conversations displayed a "down-regulated inflammatory response," meaning they had healthier immune systems and were less likely to suffer from inflammatory conditions like hypertension and heart disease.

This was kind of a big deal. And Mehl believes it has some huge implications. For one thing, it means doctors can use the way you speak as a diagnostic tool. The words we use might offer clues to problems in our immune system. In effect, doctors could use language to peer into our brains and bodies to see what's going on. "Our bodily states are not readily accessible to us, but maybe we express some of that subtly in our language, and maybe we can trace that," Mehl says.

But this creates an even more tantalizing possibility: Could we make ourselves healthier by going out and having good conversations about meaningful, substantive things? Can we use speech as medicine? "We know you can take ibuprofen to get an anti-inflammatory response. So, could you take a few good conversations to get an anti-inflammatory response? That's the idea," Mehl says. "There's a ton more work to be done. But language is a window into our psychological processes, and now we know it's also a window into the biological." This may sound far-fetched, but Mehl points out that speech is so central to our lives that it would be more far-fetched if speech did not have connections to physical health.

We know what good conversations are. But how can we measure if we're having enough of them? Turns out we might use our smartphones or smartwatches to keep track of what we're talking about and calculate a score. Twenty years ago, Mehl's EAR device was a clunky contraption—a mini cassette recorder with a timer. Today, EAR is just a piece of software, an app you can put on a smartphone.

Mehl is working with a software developer and a team of researchers at Harvard to squeeze that code down so that EAR can run on a smartwatch. The Harvard doctors are working with stroke patients, who recover faster if they do more talking and socializing. A talk-tracker watch would chart how much they're talking and what kind of conversations they're having. The researchers have built a prototype, but it still needs more work. The biggest challenge is how to squeeze the app's code into the tiny memory of the watch's computer. "We have watches than can count our steps and measure our sleep quality. But an equally important social behavior is how much we socialize and what kind of conversations we're having. Yet we don't have any way to track speech the way we track sleep and exercise. It's a complete blind spot," Mehl says.

It's not much of a leap to imagine talk tracking becoming mainstreamed into ordinary consumer devices, or our watch giving us a gentle nudge to get up from our desks and go talk to someone.

THE "I" OF THE STORM

Once again using the EAR device, Mehl joined a team that made a third big discovery: that people who suffer from anxiety and depression use the first-person singular pronouns *I*, *me*, and *my* more than other people. What was once believed to be a sign of narcissism is actually an indication of negative emotional states. Researchers call this kind of speaking "I-talk," and say it's a marker for "negative affect," which encompasses anxiety, depression, and stress. The report's lead author, Allison Tackman, a psychologist at the University of Arizona, even narrowed things down, finding that the words *I* and *me* are correlated with negative affect more than *my*, probably because the possessive pronoun connects to something or someone else other than oneself. Of the 16,000 words we speak on average every day, about 1,400 are first-person singular pronouns. But people who are stressed out, anxious, or depressed might say *I* and *me* up to 2,000 times a day.

Psychologists use I-talk as a diagnostic tool, an indicator that someone is in emotional distress. Think about the last time you went through something stressful or agonizing—a breakup, getting fired from your job—and how, in your "woe is me" phase, you turned all your attention inward. Why did this happen to *me*? What's wrong with *me*? What did *I* do wrong? Why can't *I* get better? Why don't you like *me*? You're caught in the vortex of what Mehl calls "the metaphorical *I* of the storm."

If I-talk indicates depression, could you jump-start yourself out of depression by doing less of it? Mehl's mentor, James Pennebaker, a research psychologist at the University of Texas at Austin, theorized that you could. Pennebaker made his name studying pronouns. His big discovery was that the words someone uses—particularly the pronouns—reveal what makes that person tick. Want to predict how well a kid will do in college, or whether a politician is likely to lead a country into war? It's all encoded in their speech, Pennebaker declared.

In the 1990s, Pennebaker came up with an idea he called "pronoun therapy," in which he instructed people to monitor their use of the first-person singular and try to avoid it. The results were mixed, probably because focusing so much on not saying *I* takes your attention away from the actual conversation you're having.

Since then, however, others have found that small language changes can indeed help people regulate negative emotions. A Harvard study found that therapy patients who reduced their use of *I* and, oddly enough, cut down on using present-tense verbs—a technique called "linguistic distancing"—improved their psychological health. Researchers at the University of Michigan found that using a technique called "distanced self-talk"—talking to yourself in the second or third person or using your own name, and avoiding *I* and *me*—had similar effects. The Michigan psychologists concluded that therapists might use distanced self-talk as a technique to help people process stressful or negative experiences, as "subtle shifts in language can be leveraged to adaptively alter a person's self-perspective in ways that have implications for how they think and feel."

Those researchers are talking about therapists taking these approaches with patients, but maybe it's worth trying them on our own. It's impossible never to use the words *I*, *me*, and *my*, but spending a day keeping those words to a minimum—engaging in pronoun therapy—is a worthwhile exercise. In the spirit of STFU, you are forcing yourself to think about how you speak and to be intentional in your word choice as you employ the linguistic distancing technique. It feels weird to spend time talking to yourself in the second or third person or to use your own name instead of using *I* and *me*. But distanced self-talk is something you can practice when you're alone. And the real benefit might just come from slowing down enough to think about how you are speaking.

FOREST BATHING: THE CALL OF THE MILD

I did not tell many people that I was going forest bathing. Most of my friends do not go in for the crystal-wearing, consciousness-raising, tree-hugging, sacred-ritual-in-the-woods stuff, and I knew what they would say if I had told them about my plans: *What's next? Listening to Enya? Finding a shaman? Going vegan? Birkenstocks?* One of my friends, a techie in San Francisco, laughed out loud when I told him.

My guide was Todd Lynch, a friendly, soft-spoken guy in his fifties who works as a landscape architect and artist. We met in the parking lot near the entrance to a forest in the Berkshires and headed off into the woods. I had found Todd on a website that lists hundreds of certified forest bathing guides in the United States. I was hoping that a few hours soaking up nature might do something to mitigate my overtalking affliction—that if I could force myself to STFU for three hours in the woods, I might bring the habit to the rest of my life.

Forest bathing originated in Japan, where they call it *shinrin-yoku.* In the early 1980s, doctors started looking for ways to deal with the problem of overworked city dwellers keeling over from heart attacks and came up with an idea: go walk around in a forest. Since then, Japan has built hundreds of specially designated forest bathing trails all over the country. The Japanese see forest bathing as serious medicine. The website for the Japan National Tourism Organization devotes an entire section to forest bathing and where to do it in Japan—like the Akasawa forest, where *shinrin-yoku* began. The coolest forest bathing itinerary takes you on a trek through sacred sites in the forests of the Kii Peninsula and includes a stay at a Shinto temple, where you can spend an overnight living like a monk.

The godfather of forest bathing, Dr. Qing Li, a medical school professor in Japan, has been doing studies for the past two decades and has found demonstrable health benefits to forest bathing, which can be quantified and measured. He claims that forest bathing works because trees release phytoncides, natural oils that protect them from bugs and bacteria. Phytoncides have scents—think of the smells of cypress, eucalyptus, and pine. Li's research has found that phytoncides cause the body to increase the production of anticancer proteins and natural killer (NK) cells, which fight off intruders like viruses and tumors. He claims that one forest bathing trip per month is enough to keep your NK cells at a high level.

In one study, Li found that people who spent two hours forest bathing increased their sleep time by 15 percent. They also had lower levels of the stress hormones cortisol and adrenaline, lower blood pressure, more energy, and less depression. One Japanese study found that a full day of forest bathing "demonstrated significant positive effects on mental health, especially in those with depressive tendencies." Li claims that one phytoncide, D-limonene, is more effective at improving mood than antidepressants. "There is no medicine you can take that has such a direct influence on your health as a walk in a beautiful forest," he writes in *Forest Bathing: How Trees Can Help You Find Health and Happiness.*

The first rule of forest bathing is that you walk . . . very . . . slowly. Todd and I probably took thirty minutes to travel a few hundred yards into the woods. Then we sat down in a clearing and did more or less nothing except listen to birds and watch treetops swaying in the wind. Nothing really happened—but that's the whole point. After three hours, Todd and I had a little tea ceremony, walked back

out to the parking lot, and said our goodbyes. I don't know
if anything happened to my blood pressure or white blood
cell count, but I drove home feeling great, my senses height-
ened. Everything looked a little more vivid. It reminded me
of the day when I first got eyeglasses and rode home marveling at a world I had never seen before. I had not taken
my phone with me to the woods, and after returning I had
no interest in checking to see if I had missed anything. I
turned the radio off and made the two-hour drive home in
silence, imagining those phytoncides coursing through my
bloodstream, working their magic and cranking out fresh
battalions of NK cells.

Li's studies proving the efficacy of forest bathing on
physical and emotional well-being jibe with other research
showing that silence appears to act like medicine for the
brain, helping it generate new neurons. This "neurogenesis" creates greater resiliency and reduces anxiety in
stressful situations. That's the good news. The bad news is
that, so far, the research applies only to mice, which don't
have as many brain cells as we do. Still, some scientists suspect the results might lead to therapies to help people who
suffer from anxiety and do not respond well to antidepressants. Instead of Zoloft, we might try a doctor-supervised
dose of STFU.

The idea that spending time in nature improves our
health and well-being made perfect sense to Harvard biologist Edward O. Wilson, who hypothesized that our affinity
for the outdoors and love of living things have been hard-
wired into our DNA by evolution and exist as innate parts
of our psychological and physiological makeup. Wilson
calls this "biophilia," a name derived from the ancient

Greek words for "life" and "love." It's the reason people watch birds, melt at the sight of baby bunnies, travel to Yellowstone National Park to marvel at the bison, and rush to the window when a deer wanders into their yard. It's why walking through Muir Woods among giant thousand-year-old redwood trees takes your breath away. Other living things, flora or fauna, tug at something inside us.

Monks, those masters of silence, live five years longer on average than men in the general population, according to Marc Luy, a demographer in Vienna who has spent more than a decade poring through records from cloisters in Bavaria from 1890 to the present—a monk-like endeavor in its own right. "Silence is definitely one aspect that reduces [the monks'] stress factor," Luy told me. "Silence might not explain everything, but that time when you are by yourself, when you don't deal with things other than grace and prayer and thoughts, that's an important part of reducing stress."

Over the past decade, forest bathing has become a global phenomenon and a booming business. Finland opened a "well-being forest trail" in 2010. There are so-called power forests throughout Europe, all part of a rising interest in eco-health tourism. Europe got a head start on the healing power of nature—think of those German hot springs towns whose names begin with "Bad," or the town of Spa, in Belgium.

In the United States, forest bathing boomed during the pandemic, says Amos Clifford, a wilderness guide and psychotherapist in Arizona who developed a three-hour forest bathing program and created a company, the Association of Nature and Forest Therapy Guides and Programs, that trains people to become certified forest bathing guides. More than 1,700 people in sixty-two countries have become ANFT certified—nearly four hundred of them in 2021 alone. In the United States, there are more than a thousand people certified as guides. They include physicians, pastors, and psychotherapists.

They're all listed on the ANFT website, and most have their own websites where you can book forest bathing trips. They also all follow Clifford's three-hour forest bathing program, which he calls "relational forest therapy." Clifford believes that a lot of our problems originate in our being estranged from nature and, thus, estranged from ourselves. While Japanese forest bathing takes a more scientific approach and is centered on the medicinal benefits of phytoncides, Clifford's program is more about psychology.

For some people, forest bathing is just a way to chill out in the woods. But other people find themselves dredging up some heavy memories and emotions and have a deeper, almost transformative experience. "We get a certain amount of people who show up thinking it's just some hippie bullshit," Clifford said. "Oddly enough, the ones who are most skeptical are the ones who are most likely to come back in tears."

You don't necessarily need to hire a guide. You can learn a lot just by reading Clifford's book, *Your Guide to Forest Bathing: Experience the Healing Power of Nature*, or Qing Li's *Forest Bathing: How Trees Can Help You Find Health and Happiness*, which is pretty much the bible for forest bathing. Li says you don't even need to find a forest. You can just go to your local park.

STFU AND HEAL YOUR BRAIN

Dhiraj Rajaram is the founder and CEO of Mu Sigma, a multibillion-dollar tech company based in Bangalore, India. A few years ago, Rajaram began encouraging Mu Sigma's four thousand employees to take thirty-minute breaks at 10:30 a.m. and 3:30 p.m. and to spend that time in silence, away from their desks, computers, and smartphones. No texting, checking email, or scrolling through Twitter. "It's not just audio silence, but also video silence," Rajaram told me. He believes these breaks make people more creative and even more productive. Though employees lose an hour at their desks, "they use the remaining time of the day better."

Mu Sigma depends on the ingenuity and creativity of mathematicians and computer scientists who must find new ways to analyze enormous amounts of data so that its clients, mostly Fortune 500 companies, can make better decisions. The company describes itself as "part design studio, part research lab" and calls its analysts "decision scientists."

An engineer by training, Rajaram practices Vipassana meditation and views himself as a philosopher as much as a businessperson. He believes information overload is driving us all a little bit crazy. "The issue is not just that we talk too much. It's that we are fed so much information that we don't know what is noise and what is signal," he said.

Social media forces us to create new selves and cuts us off from our authentic selves, which interferes with creativity. "A lot of creativity comes from having an authentic connection with yourself," he said. "The issue is that we have become disconnected from ourselves. We get buried under layers of inauthenticity that society puts on us. We're all on Facebook and Instagram and LinkedIn, trying to please people."

Rajaram's silence-at-work policy was put on hold when the pandemic struck and everyone started working from home. But he believes silence and stillness are needed now more than ever. As our world keeps getting louder, we are being pushed to the brink of a crisis. "We are entering an age," he said, "in which our biggest problem is going to be mental health."

MEDITATION AS MEDICATION

Jack Dorsey is one of the most creative businesspersons in the world. He has dreamed up two of the top tech companies of the past twenty years. First was Twitter, the most important and influential social network. For most people, that would have been enough for one lifetime, but a few years after starting Twitter, Dorsey cofounded Square, which makes those little credit card readers you see everywhere, and became an even bigger success. Those companies together are worth more than one hundred billion dollars, and for years, Dorsey somehow found time to be CEO of both at the same time. But even that is not enough for Dorsey's restless imagination. He's now leaping into Bitcoin and blockchain technology, the tech industry's next big thing, and looking for new opportunities.

Dorsey's secret is that he knows how and when to STFU. He starts every day with a half hour of meditation, then walks five miles to work, which takes him just over an hour, usually in silence. When he really wants to have fun, he travels to some remote corner of the world and spends ten days doing the silent Vipassana meditation that Rajaram practices. Dorsey has claimed that this is the key to his creativity.

Science suggests that meditation makes people more creative. But there are other benefits. Buddhist monks and nuns who master the practice of meditation have better mental health, for example. Meditation can change the structure of your brain (in good ways) and slow the atrophy of gray matter as you age, making it a kind of fountain of youth. Meditation reduces anxiety and depression about as well as antidepressants, and "without the associated toxicities," doctors at Johns Hopkins reported.

Apparently, meditation shifts your brain into "default mode," where it has nothing to do, so it just sits there idling, looking for something to do. That effort of seeking some kind of stimulus or task gives your brain a workout that improves your cognitive abilities, making you better at remembering things—like where you parked your car in that huge lot outside the mall—and better able to think about the future. The latter skill may help explain why Dorsey keeps coming up with ideas for things that nobody else has even imagined, like a network where hundreds of millions of people can keep track of what's going on in the world, in real time, or a system that lets cab drivers and small businesses take credit card payments on an iPad.

Every time Dorsey returns from one of his ten-day Vipassana sojourns, he raves about it on Twitter, which has inspired loads of tech bros to give it a try, presumably hoping that they, too, might become billionaires. Most can't last the full ten days and peace out after a day or two. It's hard to give up those phones and laptops. And Vipassana is not relaxing. It's incredibly painful to sit in the lotus position for hours, but the pain is considered part of the process.

There are 25 places in the United States that offer Vipassana retreats, 362 worldwide. All kinds of meditation retreats are popping up, and some have long wait-lists. Vision quests are becoming so mainstream that *Inc.* magazine touts them to aspiring entrepreneurs. Partly due to the stress of the Covid-19 lockdown, meditation apps have become a billion-dollar business. More than 2,500 of them have been released since 2015. One popular app, Calm, provides music and sounds, like falling rain, and can also tell you bedtime stories to help you fall asleep. Another, Headspace, lets you tailor your program to meet certain goals, like improving your creativity or becoming more patient.

People are shutting up all over the place—believing, like Jack Dorsey, that taking a break from the world can improve their ability to operate within it.

APPLYING THE FIVE WAYS TO STFU

I think of the Five Ways to STFU as a workout, just like going for a run, hitting the gym, or doing yoga. It's a daily practice. Once you get into the habit, it gets easier. In general, it's all about slowing down, speaking with intention, letting other people speak, asking good questions, and then really listening to the response. Just like hitting the gym, you're doing exercises that will make you healthier and happier.

"When possible, say nothing" is the most powerful of the Five Ways to STFU. Choose a specific conversation today and focus on finding spaces where you can say nothing. You're not being rude; you're being polite. It's easiest to do this with strangers. Resist the urge to strike up a conversation with your waiter. Do not seek to learn the life story of your Uber driver. Let the nice barista ring you up and get back to work. Zoom meetings provide another great opportunity to practice.

Cut back on small talk by playing the "Is that a question?" game. When you're doing an errand or making an appointment to get a haircut, resolve that you will speak only if you're asked a direct question, and that, when you are asked a question, you will answer as succinctly as possible. I have a habit of turning any encounter into an opportunity for chitchat. If I'm checking out at the grocery store or badging in at the gym, whichever poor soul happens to be there is fair game. I also have the habit of turning a "yes" answer into a long disquisition about how and why I have arrived at some decision, when a simple one-word answer would do. The "Is that a question?" game has really helped me curb this impulse. Practicing in low-stakes situations has helped me get better at using it in places where it really matters, like at work.

Master the power of the pause by letting silences hang in conversations. It feels awkward at first, and you will have an impulse to jump in quickly to fill the void. Over time, it gets easier. Pauses are a big part of having those "meaningful, substantive conversations" that are key to emotional and physical well-being. Before you speak, take a breath and wait two beats.

Seek out silence, and you will find yourself feeling calmer but also more refreshed, with more energy and a greater capacity to be creative. Microsoft cofounder Bill Gates retreats alone twice a year to a cabin in a forest for a "Think Week," where he disconnects from electronics and reads books and research papers. Even quick opportunities— a few minutes at work with no phone, no computer, no music—can recharge your brain battery. If you're struggling to solve a problem, get up, walk away, and do *not* think about that problem. Go for a walk. Set up a forest bathing appointment. Sit quietly and let your mind wander and drift. Think about those studies that found that silence causes you to grow new brain cells. Close your eyes and feel those neurons springing to life.

You might feel bored—and if so, that's great. Periods of boredom are gifts from the universe. You're not wasting time; you're seizing an opportunity. The philosopher Bertrand Russell believed that "fructifying boredom" is a wellspring of creativity. "A generation that cannot endure boredom will be a generation . . . in which every vital impulse slowly withers, as though they were cut flowers in a vase," he wrote.

Russell may have been onto something. Researchers have found that doing something boring makes people more creative. They suspect it might be because the brain, when bored, goes looking for things to do. It feels unsatisfied, so it goes into Search mode. Thanks to smartphones, we can keep ourselves from ever being bored. There's always a distraction. But that distraction is unproductive. Our brains become occupied with empty activity, which leaves no room for daydreaming or creative thinking.

Another idea: Keep a talk journal. Dieters keep food journals where they write down everything they eat. STFU practitioners can do something similar, spending some time at the end of the day to think back on the conversations they had. How many were meaningful? How often were you able to really listen? Did you have one conversation that went really well? If so, how did you accomplish this? Writing this down will reinforce the habits you are trying to cultivate.

This sounds like a lot of work, but so is going to the gym—and the payoff from STFU is easier to obtain than six-pack abs. You'll feel happier, calmer, more in control, more optimistic, and less anxious. You'll also sleep better. You may even find that you're less prone to angry outbursts and catastrophizing.

The physical benefits—new brain cells, a stronger immune system, reduced likelihood of developing heart disease—are not as readily apparent, but I've decided to trust the science and take that part on faith.

6

STFU AT WORK

Business is changing. Work is changing. In the old way of doing things, companies were loud. They bought ads, invented slogans, splattered the world with messaging. Business was all about broadcasting, boasting, barraging, bullshitting—jumping up and down, waving your arms, shouting for attention. Employees behaved the same way: build the brand of You, advertise your talents to your boss and to the world, seek attention on social media.

New Business has flipped that script. Instead of blasting messages at customers and trying to persuade them to buy the product you have made, you listen to them and find out what they need. Product development is about iteration and collaboration, running experiments, failing fast, and learning from mistakes.

This new way of business is being driven in part by the shift from selling goods to selling services. In the goods-based world, you built something and then tried to find customers for it. In the service economy, you find customers first and then build solutions to their problems. It's called "working backward from the customer."

Everything is becoming a service. Software, computing power, and storage are sold as services. Automakers once talked about selling cars, but now they realize that they're not selling cars; they're selling transportation, which is a different thing altogether. In the world of transportation as a service, cars are just computers on wheels, and the money comes not from "moving the iron," but from selling software and services delivered through the vehicles' digital dashboards. Even General Electric, an industrial conglomerate that builds jet engines and wind turbines, now bills itself as an "as-a-service" company.

Service requires humility, and the everything-as-a-service economy requires a new kind of leader. The boss used to be an alpha who barked out orders like a marine drill sergeant at Parris Island, a commander in chief who knew all the answers. Now we're in the age of humble leaders, quiet leaders, leaders who ask a lot of questions and lead by following—in short, STFU leaders. Hal Gregersen, director of the MIT Leadership Center, interviewed two hundred CEOs and found that many live in what he calls "the CEO bubble," where they get only good news and fail to anticipate problems. But great innovators like Apple founder and CEO Steve Jobs and Amazon founder and chairman Jeff Bezos break through the bubble by knowing when to STFU and ask questions. Gregersen created the 4-24 Project, suggesting that business leaders spend four minutes out of every twenty-four hours, which works out to one full day a year, doing nothing but asking questions. In a world driven by artificial intelligence and machine learning, where systems are more intelligent than the humans running them, know-it-all leaders are as ridiculous and obsolete as business cards and paper Rolodexes.

STFU leaders are satellite dishes, not broadcast antennae: they listen more than they speak. They also know enough to know what they don't know, and they win by being able to soak up information and then adapt and respond faster than their competitors. Underlistening is the flip side of overtalking, and just as deadly.

STFU IN PRODUCT DEVELOPMENT

Over the past decade, many companies have adopted the Lean methodology, a way of designing new products that is all about listening. Lean uses a build-measure-learn cycle in which you build a "minimum viable product," listen to customer feedback, then use that feedback to build the next version of the product. The key word is *listen*. And the listening is constant. In the world of Lean, there is no such thing as a finished product. Every product keeps being refined and improved even after it ships, with new features added to adapt to changing customer needs. Everything is a work in progress.

Twilio, a software company in San Francisco, updates its software every week. The company talks about listening as "having your face in the place," which means sending engineers out to sit with customers and see how they do their jobs. On the wall of every meeting room at Twilio you will find a pair of shoes that a customer has sent to the company—a constant reminder that employees need to "walk in the customer's shoes."

Bunq, a mobile banking company in the Netherlands,

gets a lot of ideas from its customer service department. Reps there solve customer problems and then tell software developers what they need to change or add. Every few weeks, Bunq's software developers walk to a local train station and ask random people to look at prototypes and give their opinion. Bunq updates its app every week, usually making two to three small changes but occasionally adding a big new feature. The product never stays the same for long.

The same goes for Tesla: the car you bought last month is not the car you're driving today, and the car you drive next month will not be the car you're driving today. That's because Tesla constantly pushes over-the-air software updates to its cars, adding new features all the time rather than waiting for the next new model to come out in a few years. In a sense, there is no such thing as a finished Tesla. The company figures out which new features to add by pulling data from its cars and "listening" to its customers.

Tesla also takes an STFU approach to marketing and advertising—by never spending a dime on it and instead plowing that budget into research and development. In 2020, Tesla CEO Elon Musk got rid of his public relations team, which had been another waste of money, in his opinion. In public, Musk is an obnoxious loudmouth and overtweeting bully, but some say that behind the scenes he is a good listener when he huddles with his engineers to solicit feedback and talk about developing products. "If you pose to Elon a serious question, he'll consider it. And he'll kind of go into this almost like a trance—he'll stare off into space and you can see the wheels turning. And he's focusing all his intellect, which is considerable, on this one question," Garrett Reisman, an engineer at one of Musk's other companies, SpaceX, once said.

Tesla's never-selling-but-always-listening-and-always-changing business model has radically challenged the auto industry, and the same challenge is coming to every industry: finance, health care, retail. In this world of constant iteration, the ability to listen to customers and use their feedback is the skill most crucial to success, and one that has made Musk the richest person in the world.

The same soft skills and humility that define leadership in the world of New Business are required in every role, in every part of the business, from top leaders to middle managers to individual contributors. Talking less, listening more, speaking with intention, and asking good questions have become crucial to success. Hard skills mattered a lot in a world where you did one job for your entire career, but not so much in a world where you might have a dozen or more jobs before you call it quits. The new world is all about listening and learning.

STFU IN SALES

Sales might once have been a contest of domination, where those who succeeded were glib backslappers who wined and dined their clients and slick-talked and arm-twisted customers into buying things they didn't want or need. Today, sales is more about listening than talking. Top performers ask questions, define problems, and devise ways to solve them.

A company called Gong uses machine learning software that analyzes sales calls to find out what works and what doesn't. Its software vacuums up millions of hours of audio data and then analyzes it to figure out how the best sales reps operate. Gong's customers use this information to train new sales reps and help underperformers improve.

In 2017 Gong analyzed more than five hundred thousand calls and found that sales calls with the best close rates were ones in which reps knew how to STFU and ask questions instead of making a sales pitch. To be precise, the most successful reps asked eleven to fourteen questions. Fewer than that, and you're not digging deep enough. More than that, and the call starts to feel like an interrogation.

Gong's machine learning also deduced that calls work best when the questions are scattered throughout and when a rep identifies three to four specific problems—no more, no fewer—that the customer needs to solve. The best reps made calls feel like conversations, spending 54 percent of the call listening and 46 percent talking. The worst reps talked 72 percent of the time.

Slick talkers and arm twisters don't do well in the era of STFU sales.

STFU IN CUSTOMER SERVICE

The average person will spend forty-three days of their life on hold. That's roughly a month and a half. Why? Because the people ahead of them in the queue won't STFU. The average customer service call lasts two minutes longer than it needs to, according to Myra Golden, a customer service guru. All those wasted minutes add up. Golden teaches call center workers at big companies—Coca-Cola, McDonald's, Walmart—how to claw back that lost time by getting callers to STFU. The way to make callers talk less, she says, is to master your own ability to STFU. Resist the urge to argue with angry people or to have conversations with the friendly ones who want to talk about their families and ask you how you're doing today. Both these types, the shouters and the overtalkers, are time wasters, and both need to be coerced into shutting up. Golden's rule with the friendly folks: Keep things tight but polite, give limited responses, and keep driving the caller back to the matter at hand. Say as little as possible, and do not provide excessive information: "I'm doing well, thank you for asking. Now what's going on, and how can I help you?"

With angry callers who are lying or exaggerating— "I've been on hold for thirty minutes!" says the guy who has been on hold for four—let it slide. Don't get into a debate or argument. If they want to vent, let them vent. Golden says most people wind down after about thirty seconds. Once they do, seize control by hitting them with three short, close-ended questions regarding the topic under discussion. *What is your rental agreement number? What is the invoice number? What is the date on the agreement?* It doesn't matter what the questions are. By forcing the customer to make three short statements that are factual rather than emotional, you're helping them calm down and training them to STFU. Once you have gained control of the conversation, you can solve their problem and move on to the next call. The art of doing this well begins with knowing how to control your own emotions and speak with intention—to STFU. For what it's worth, the same techniques apply when you're the customer who is calling for service or support. Keep it short, don't vent, and know exactly what you want, and you'll have a better experience.

And you will be helping yourself and everyone else reclaim some of those forty-three days spent listening to hold music and getting angry.

STFU AS A NEGOTIATION TOOL

Pauses in conversation make people feel uncomfortable. And it doesn't take long. A team of researchers in the Netherlands found that it takes only four seconds for people to start to feel "distressed, afraid, hurt, and rejected." That distress and discomfort make silence a powerful negotiation weapon. "I'm constantly amazed by what will happen if you don't speak over what will happen if you do," says Gavin Presman, a sales and negotiation consultant in London.

Presman told me about an executive from an Italian conglomerate who was trying to persuade a sheikh in the United Arab Emirates to give his company exclusive access to the local market. As Presman tells the story, "The Italian executive goes in and says, 'Okay, so this is the deal.' The sheikh goes, 'That doesn't seem right to me.' The Italian doesn't respond. He just sits there. This goes on for *twenty-five minutes*. It's killing him, but he forces himself to sit there, looking calm. Finally, the sheikh says, 'Okay. I will do business with you.'"

Mastering the power of the pause can also get you a better salary. In fact, the biggest mistake job seekers make when they are negotiating their salary is that "they don't know how to shut up," says Katie Donovan, who runs a consultancy in Boston called Equal Pay Negotiations, whose mission is to keep people, especially women, from being shortchanged. A big part of Donovan's coaching involves teaching job seekers to develop the discipline to use silence to gain leverage in negotiations. It's not easy, because most people find long pauses awkward and uncomfortable.

"We hate silence. We feel there is a necessity to fill it in," Donovan told me one night over dinner and drinks in Boston's Seaport neighborhood. But if you give in, you've already lost. People actually end up negotiating against themselves. Donovan describes a common scenario: The recruiter makes an offer and then goes silent. The job seeker is disappointed in the offer, but then, getting nervous because of the silence, starts inventing reasons to accept it. People will actually start doing the recruiter's job, listing all the reasons they should accept the low offer: *It's a better commute. There's room for growth, a chance to learn new skills. It will look good on my résumé.* "This happens every day of the week," Donovan says. "The thing I'm teaching people is to stop negotiating against themselves. That's the main problem you fix by telling people to shut up."

She offers an example of how to get what you deserve. Early in her career, Donovan was offered a job and was negotiating her salary. The VP doing the hiring played a common negotiating trick, where you build urgency by setting a deadline. He set the meeting at 4:00 p.m. on a Friday—a classic HR pressure move—and made her an offer, but added that "I need an answer today." Donovan said she would consider the offer and get back to him next week. Then—this is the key—she did not stand up. She just sat there. The pause became uncomfortable. She forced herself not to give in. Finally, the VP broke. He increased his offer, but again said it was good only if she gave him an answer right away. "I appreciate the offer," Donovan said. "I'll think about it and get back to you next week." Then, once again, she went silent and just sat there. The VP left the office. A few minutes later, he came back with a higher offer. This one was 20 percent above his original offer.

She took the job.

"If you want something," Donovan says, "do it quietly. That's how you get the result you need."

TAKE A LESSON FROM STEVE JOBS

If you want a master class in how to give a presentation, go to YouTube and watch the 2007 event where Apple CEO Steve Jobs introduced the iPhone, the most important product in Apple's history. A lot of keynote speakers bound out onto the stage to some kind of high-energy music like game show hosts, with big smiles and lots of arm-waving, trying to get the audience revved up. Jobs does the opposite. He walks out in silence. There's no music. The auditorium is so quiet that you can hear his New Balance sneakers touch the stage as he takes each step. He does not smile. He does not even look at the audience. He looks down at his hands, like a monk in meditation, lost in thought. He takes eight steps. It takes him eight full seconds to do this. Then he turns to the audience and delivers one line:

"This is a day," he says, pausing, "I've been looking forward to," he says, pausing, "for two and a half years."

Then he stops again and pauses—for another six seconds.

And you're hooked. You can't look away. You hang on his every word.

Jobs rehearsed his presentations obsessively, practicing every step and gesture, and paying as much attention to

the spaces between the words as he did to the words themselves. What's more interesting is that he was nothing like
his onstage persona. Offstage, he was a shouter: impulsive,
loud, hotheaded, prone to rage. But he mastered the art of
using pauses and dead space when giving a talk. And you
can do the same.

Even if you're just giving a PowerPoint presentation
to a few people at work, insert a few seconds of STFU.
It's not easy to do this. It goes against everything in our
nature. The second you look out at people who are sitting
there looking at you, your blood pressure goes up and your
heart rate increases. Your body starts producing adrenaline. Your brain wants you to say something, anything. But
don't. Count a few seconds. You don't have to go for eight
seconds, the way Jobs did, but you want people to notice
the emptiness and lean toward you. That way they will
hear what you say and remember it.

Jobs understood that talking well means talking less.
He was a ruthless editor, constantly trying to convey his
ideas in as few words as possible. He also understood that
the spaces between the words are as important as the words
themselves.

OVERTALKING IS A CAREER KILLER

A friend of mine has had eleven jobs in the past fifteen
years. One job lasted five months. Another lasted eight.
My friend has an MBA from a top university. But she's a
Blurter, and her colleagues think she's obnoxious. Once,
she was talking with a group of coworkers and the discussion turned to sriracha sauce and all the cool ways you can
use it.

"But do you know what you *shouldn't* use sriracha for?" one guy asked.

"Masturbation?" Robin blurted.

Crickets. Nobody laughed. In less than a year, she moved on to her next place of employment. She didn't lose the job because of the sriracha wisecrack, but there were probably dozens more like it. Blurters tend to be highly intelligent and quick thinking, but they're too fast, and they lack a filter. Their brains generate an idea and *whoosh*—out it flies! Even when they do understand that a comment is not going to go over well, they can't resist saying it. Over time, those little zingers and off-color remarks start to add up.

People who can't STFU in the workplace are hated by their coworkers, who pray for the days when an overtalker doesn't come to the office. That was the conclusion of a research report done by University of Nebraska graduate student Jason Axsom. People "celebrate these days of freedom and comment to one another about how peaceful the office is during the compulsive talker's absence." In every job he ever had, Axsom said there was at least one compulsive talker who made everyone else miserable. He believed the problem was widespread and hoped that if overtalkers could see the pain they were inflicting on others, they might be motivated to change.

"I thought maybe we could help compulsive talkers, that maybe if we could understand them, we could coach them and guide them so they could get help for their compulsive behaviors," Axsom told me. "If we could demonstrate how potentially damaging this behavior could be to your career, then the solutions might follow." Unfortunately, nobody has ever come up with a course of therapy for overtalkers, who continue to roam the corporate world, leaving misery and lost productivity in their wake.

Axsom's paper has been downloaded nearly two thousand times, an extraordinary figure for a grad school thesis and an indication of just how many people out there are looking for ways to deal with workplace overtalkers short of cutting out their tongues. For the report, Axsom interviewed fifteen people who worked in marketing, banking, teaching, accounting, advertising, and retail sales. Some were high-ranking executives; others rank-and-file hourly employees. Some worked in Fortune 500 companies; others in small businesses. One was a professor. They all described coworkers who wandered the halls searching for new victims, like zombies hunting fresh brains. These talkaholic colleagues told the same stories over and over. They overshared in ways that were uncomfortable, and not just about themselves but about their friends and relatives, complete strangers. There were no limits. These compulsive talkers lacked the ability to pick up on social cues. Their coworkers could open their laptops and start typing, and the talkaholic would keep talking.

Talkaholics often make a good first impression, Axsom found. They're gregarious. They're funny. They like to give presentations, and they're great storytellers. After all, they've had more practice than most people. "The pattern I noticed across all the subjects was that, at the beginning, the person seemed very likable," Axsom told me. "And they were viewed as competent and intelligent. But as time goes on, the stories start getting repeated, and people start losing productivity. They go from thinking that this person is friendly to thinking, *This has to stop*. And they start perceiving the person as less intelligent."

Thus, compulsive talkers are less likely to be promoted: "The compulsive behavior will eventually trap the overtalker into their current positions without the opportunity for advancement," Axsom wrote. Compulsive talkers become pariahs. Even people who originally liked them start avoiding them. Coworkers invent fake meetings. They run in the other direction or ask to be moved to a different cubicle.

The tragedy is that some talkaholics refuse to change. Axsom tells the story of a man who was promoted to manage a five-person team. He was talented, but he was also a Blabber. He constantly talked to his team, rambling about whatever happened to be floating across his mind that day. The manager thought he was being a good boss. Meanwhile, his team wanted to throw him off the roof of the building. They spent so much time enduring his monologues that they couldn't get their work done. Some became so frustrated that they started looking for new jobs. Finally, they complained to management, and the overtalking boss was given a choice: learn how to STFU or lose the manager position. Here's the amazing thing: *He chose the demotion*. He was so addicted to overtalking that instead of getting help for his talkaholism, he torpedoed his career.

What stands out most in the Axsom report is the tone of desperation and suffering in the voices of the interview subjects. Many turned their interviews into therapy sessions. "People were so anxious to talk. They would talk for more than an hour, pouring their hearts out," Axsom recalls. They described feeling trapped, like prisoners, unable to escape their tormentor. Some prayed that their overtalker would be fired, or considered quitting just to get away from them. "Please take them away," one woman pleaded. Axsom was struck by the depth of their responses: "I felt bad in a way, because they were asking me to help them, but I didn't have any answers. I still don't."

STFU IN MEETINGS

There are two kinds of people: the ones who like meetings and the ones who are sane. Right now, the first kind are winning.

Americans suffer through more than eleven million meetings per day, more than a billion per year. Only 11 percent of them are productive. One study found that the average worker attends sixty-two meetings each month and that participants claimed that half the meetings were a complete waste of time, while 39 percent of people admitted to having *slept* during meetings. The problem keeps getting worse: the time people spend in meetings has been growing 8 to 10 percent each year since 2020. One-on-one meetings have increased 500 percent in just the past two years, and not coincidentally, the average workday has increased 1.4 hours. We're now averaging 44.6 hours a week.

This is insane. Meetings are probably the biggest opportunity to apply STFU in the workplace. Here are some ways to do it:

Keep meetings small. The value of a meeting decreases in direct proportion to the square of the number of participants. Amazon follows a policy called the "two-pizza rule," which means if you need more than two pizzas to feed everyone in the meeting, you have too many people. That works out to about ten people, max.

If you're asked to attend a big meeting, do whatever you can to avoid it. If you can't avoid the meeting, at least resist the urge to add to the pointless verbiage. And don't be afraid to bail. "Walk out of a meeting or drop off a call as soon as it is obvious you aren't adding value," Tesla CEO Elon Musk advises. "It is not rude to leave, it is rude to make someone stay and waste their time."

Keep meetings short. A lot of us default to thirty-minute meetings, but the ideal meeting length is fifteen minutes. In those first fifteen minutes, 91 percent of people will be paying attention, but this percentage drops off as the meeting goes on.

Just say no. Just because you've been invited to a group meeting it doesn't mean you have to attend. It takes courage to turn someone down, but adding an explanation— "I'm super busy, but I'll listen to the recording later"—can get you off the hook.

Use the WAIT methodology. Before you speak in a meeting, ask yourself, *Why am I talking?* You can also ask yourself these questions:

- *What purpose will this comment serve?*
- *Will I move the conversation forward?*
- *Am I providing an answer to someone's question?*
- *Is what I want to say important?*
- *Is this the time and place to bring it up?*
- *Am I expressing an opinion or stating a fact?*

- *Have I thought this through well enough?*
- *Can I say this concisely?*
- *Is it my turn to speak?*
- *Am I the right person to make this point, or should I encourage someone else to speak?*
- *Has someone else said this already?*
- *Am I talking because I believe I am required to say something?*
- *Am I trying to impress people?*
- *If this thought does not get expressed, will it make any difference?*

Not many comments can pass the WAIT test, which means you are going to spend a lot of time in meetings saying nothing. The trick is to do this without zoning out. Make a point of paying attention to whoever is speaking. Lean into the conversation. Take notes. Smile. Nod in agreement. Use your body language and facial expressions to show people (or pretend) that you are engaged.

Pass the ball quickly. Pro soccer players keep the ball moving. You can do the same in a meeting. "Catch the pass" by acknowledging what the person before you said. Then add something brief—don't hog the ball—and toss to a teammate.

Send an email instead. The most common complaint people make about meetings is that they could have been an email. Do you really need to haul everyone into a Zoom call to get feedback on a document or give people a status update? A lot of what you need to say can be done with a quick email or a group Slack message.

HOW TO SHUT DOWN AN OVERTALKER

Once you've mastered the art of STFU in work situations, you end up creating a new problem: you can't stand the other overtalkers.

Now you need a new skill, which is how to get other people to STFU. A recent Harvard psychology study found that nearly two-thirds of conversations run longer than one of the participants wants. If you're now the master of STFU, you're going to be that person who's itching to get away.

How do you do it? Communication researchers suggest using "closing rituals" and "verbal gambits" like "It's been great talking to you," "I have to hop on a call at three," or more subtle cues, like "So, anyway . . ." You can also start making it clear that you're not really listening: "Uh-huh. Yeah. Right." But these techniques are tactical and presuppose that you're talking to a normal person. With chronic, hardcore overtalkers, you're up against a more formidable foe and must resort to one of the following stronger measures:

The sneak attack. This is a bit self-serving on my part. Just leave a copy of this book on the overtalker's desk. Bookmark this page. And/or: do the same with Jason Axsom's report on how overtalkers are perceived in the workplace.

Run. If you're confronted with an Ego Talker, escape may be your only option. You can try modest interventions, but if those fail, invent an excuse to get away. Pretend your phone is buzzing and that you need to take a call. Or don't even bother trying to be polite. "I'm sorry, I have to go" works well. It's okay to be rude. The overtalker is being selfish, and they deserve it. Besides, they're probably so wrapped up in themselves that they won't even notice. If they do notice, maybe it will help them change.

Use body language. Lean away. Turn slightly. Avoid eye contact. Pick up your phone and look at it. If you're dealing with a mild overtalker, they will likely get the hint. If not, escalate. Think of yourself as a boxer. You don't want to get trapped on the ropes. You need to keep moving. Literally lead your opponent in a circle, and gradually step away.

Interrupt. Use the same kind of body language you would use to stop an interrupter—hold up the palm, hold up an index finger.

Pump the brakes. When you're dealing with a Nervous Talker, someone who might be socially awkward and talks as a way to self-soothe, think of yourself as their helper rather than their foe. Soothe them by speaking calmly, softly, and slowly. Use your NPR voice. Start by acknowledging what they've told you, then steer them in a different direction. You're not coming to a complete stop; you're just slowing things down. "That's really interesting." Pause. "You know, there's something I've been wanting to ask you." Now you have taken control of the conversation, and you can induce them to follow your cadence. Ask a question that requires them to stop and think. "I was reading this article the other day, about how people are moving away from cities because now everybody is working remotely. Places like Bozeman, Montana, are booming. I was thinking, you know, where would I move if I could move wherever I wanted? Have you ever thought about that?"

Establish limits up front. This one works well with the dreaded airplane seatmate from hell who would talk through the whole six-hour flight if you let them. It's important to dive in right away. "I really have to catch some sleep." Or: "I'm sorry. I have a huge amount of work to finish before we land."

Build a parking lot. This is a way to keep an overtalker from hijacking the conversation in work meetings. Start by establishing what you're meeting to talk about. Anything that doesn't fit? "Let's put that in the parking lot." It's nicer than telling someone to STFU, but it means the same thing.

Talk to your overtalker. If the overtalker is a friend or family member with a chronic problem, situational interventions won't be enough. You need a permanent solution. Sit down privately and, in a calm voice, without getting angry, explain the problem and offer to help. There's a chance that your overtalker will want to change. There is also a chance that they will be offended and never talk to you again. In which case, problem solved.

Create a signal. A friend of mine developed a signal with her talkaholic husband to help him in group situations: when he started overtalking, she would place her hand gently on his. I love this technique. She didn't embarrass him or call attention to his overtalking. Instead, she offered a gesture of affection.

STFU AS A PERSONAL BRAND

Ten years ago, the cofounder of a software company told me that he measured the value of people by the number of Twitter followers they had. This seemed obviously ridiculous. Most of the CEOs of Fortune 500 companies were not on Twitter at all. How would he rate their worth? Zero? But his employees took him seriously and turned themselves into carnival barkers, posting on Twitter and Facebook, trying to build their brands. Over the course of four years, the chief marketing officer produced 225 episodes of a video podcast that nobody watched, and then he followed this up with an audio podcast that, after six years, has clawed its way up to being the 9,090th most popular podcast in the world. The social media manager fired out one tweet an hour, twenty-four hours a day—the sun never set on her empire. A team from customer service made parody videos in which they set their own lyrics to hip-hop songs and rapped about the cool, hip start-up life.

We've been sold on the idea that we need to have a personal brand, and in a world where you're going to change jobs every few years, this probably makes some sense. But we're going about it all wrong. We keep trying to rise above the noise, but as we do, we just raise the overall noise level.

Here's a novel idea. In a world where everyone is making noise, the best way to stand out might be to STFU. Build a brand around quiet competence and actual accomplishments. Be secure and confident enough in your abilities that you don't need to race around desperately seeking attention on Twitter.

There is a "chief digital evangelist" at a large software company who sometimes posts more than a hundred tweets in a single day. Nothing he tweets has anything to do with his company or the software industry. He posts insipid faux-inspirational bullshit: quotes from famous people, cute animal videos, stuff about robots, lists of attributes one needs to be successful, and his own nuggets of pseudo wisdom, like "You are not your job" and "Smart people use simple language." He's a one-man *BuzzFeed*, overtweeting an endless stream of brain manure into the hungry maw of the Twitterverse. He blasts out the same tweets over and over, probably using an automation tool. He retweets his own tweets. He has nearly six hundred thousand followers and calls himself a "Twitter celebrity." Over the past six years, he and another overtweeter, a man who describes himself as a "keynoter, futurist, and provocateur," have produced more than two hundred fifty episodes of a You-Tube show. One recent episode got eight views. Another got twenty-two.

This desperate quest for attention is starting to seem outdated and silly—just like those crazy start-up offices with the Ping-Pong tables, kooky decor, and free snacks that were all the rage a decade ago. To some extent, we were duped into Shiny New Object Syndrome. The internet gave us new ways to show off, and we decided we should use them all. The more we said, and the more places we said it, the better. Or so we thought.

Humble leaders outperform their showy counterparts. A study that tracked 120 teams comprising 495 employees found that the best teams had "leaders who demonstrate humility—through self-awareness, praising others' strengths and contributions, and being open to feedback." Humble leaders create teams that have 75 percent less stress, 50 percent higher productivity, and 40 percent less burnout. Companies are casting aside the notion of a leader as someone who is charismatic and attention seeking, who craves the spotlight, and are instead embracing the idea of leadership as a quiet, humble pursuit.

STFU leaders inspire STFU companies, as their example is driven down through the ranks. Relentless self-promoters are out. People who admit when they don't have an answer and who give credit to others are in. Humility has become such a sought-after skill that it's baked into personality assessments used by recruiters. Patagonia, the clothing company famous for its great corporate culture, screens job applicants for humility. So does Taj Hotels, a global luxury hospitality chain headquartered in Mumbai.

Soon, we may look back on the past fifteen years as an aberration, a period when the workplace temporarily lost its mind. If you really want to catch the attention of your managers and improve your chances of getting promoted, be quietly competent. Be humble. It's a rare quality these days.

Be the person on the team who knows how to STFU.

7

STFU AT HOME

My daughter was freaking out. She had a paper due for her English class in two days and had nothing to say about these poems. She was going to get a zero for the assignment, fail the class, wreck her GPA, and not get into college.

She was sixteen, a junior in high school. I wanted to fix the problem for her. I wanted to tell her how to do the assignment. That's what I had always done in the past. And guess what? It never worked. The more I tried to help, the more upset she became.

So, this time I tried something different: I sat there and STFU. I told myself to just listen to her and trust that she would figure it out on her own. It was agonizing. She was caught on the Anxiety Wheel, and the more she talked, the worse it got. The overtalker in me was dying to be let out of its cage. But I kept my resolve.

Finally, my daughter noticed that I wasn't talking and said, "What are you doing? Why are you just sitting there?"

"I'm listening," I said.

"You're not listening. You're looking at your phone."

"I'm not," I said, and pointed to my phone, which I had put on a table, out of reach.

"You're ignoring me."

"If I wanted to ignore you, I'd leave the room."

"Well, you're not helping me, so I guess you don't care," she said.

"I know you're feeling bad," I said.

"Yeah, no shit," she said.

She laughed. I did, too.

Gradually, she grew calm. The Anxiety Wheel that had been spooling up began to slow down. And then she started talking about the real problem, which was not the English paper. The real problem was that she was sixteen and adulthood was racing at her way too fast and that, like most kids her age, she was afraid she wasn't ready for it. She was about to take the SATs and apply to colleges. She was scared—not only that she might not get into college but that once she got there, she might not be able to handle it.

Just beyond that horizon looms the vast unknown of adulthood, and it's a little terrifying. You spend your whole childhood saying you can't wait to be a grown-up and get out on your own, but then you find yourself standing at the threshold—and, suddenly, you're not so sure, but it's too late. Ready or not, you can't turn back. And no one is ready.

These were not things I could fix, but she didn't want me to fix them. She just needed to be assured that it was okay to be scared and that whatever life had in store for her, she could handle it, and most important, she would not have to face it alone.

STFU: IT'S NOT JUST ABOUT YOU

The real superpower of STFU is that, in addition to help-ing yourself, you're helping other people. Making *their* lives better. Making *them* happier. STFU is about building stronger, healthier interpersonal relationships with every-one in your life.

You may start out, as I did, just hoping to rein in your compulsive talking and avoid calamities. Then you realize that there are advantages to be gained if you can STFU. You can do better in negotiations and maybe become a little bit happier, healthier, and smarter. Those things are great. But the next level is to use STFU to help your kids grow into successful adults who can solve their own prob-lems and make good decisions or to comfort a friend or relative who is going through a hard time.

Encounters like the one I had with my daughter unlock a deeper form of communication and build a stronger con-nection. You don't do much talking, but you're not passive. You're engaging in what researchers call "active silence," which sometimes can communicate more information than any number of words.

STFU as it relates to interpersonal relationships falls into two categories: strategic and tactical. Strategic conver-sations are like the one I had with my daughter, where you go after deeper, longer-term issues. Tactical conversations are where you're trying to solve the problem at hand. For example, sometimes you *do* want to help your kid figure out how to write that paper. My son is an introvert, like his mother, but if I ask open-ended questions and then get out of his way—if I resist the urge to tell him what to do and, instead, just mirror back what he says—I can get him talking.

"What are you working on these days?" I asked him one Tuesday morning as I was driving him to school.

He had this paper, he mumbled. He had written a draft, but it was terrible.

At this point, the old me might have started giving him tips and strategies for writing a paper. Instead, the new me merely asked him, "What's it about?" and let him start talking.

He spent twenty minutes explaining something called the "farming/language dispersal hypothesis," a theory that language families expanded in tandem with agriculture. I asked a few questions, recognizing that by telling the story to me, he was figuring out how to tell it in a paper. By the time I dropped him off, he had solved his problem.

It felt as if I had done nothing—because I had not said much of anything. But active silence requires effort. My silence gave him the space to work it out for himself.

Some tactical conversations evolve into strategic ones. If you can get someone talking and then get out of their way, they'll often wade into deeper waters and talk about more difficult and more important stuff. Resist the urge to offer advice. If you have had an experience similar to theirs, and you think it might be helpful for them to hear it, you can offer to tell them about it, but don't foist it on them. Let them ask. If they don't, step back.

None of this comes naturally to me. Most of my life I have done things all wrong. I cringe when I watch old home movies: all I see is a parent getting his kids wound up and overexcited. For most of my kids' lives, I have been the dad who delivered sermons and told stories, leaping from one topic to another until I got lost and asked, "Wait, what were we talking about?"

Well, *we* weren't talking about anything.

Most of us fall into the trap of talking too much to our kids; we lean in when we should sit back. But research suggests that quiet parenting works best. You do not need to have an opinion on everything. Even if you do have an opinion, you don't need to express it. Nor do you need to have all the answers. And let's be honest: we *don't* have all the answers.

Switch off your light saber and become more powerful than you can possibly imagine.

Dare to use the three most powerful parenting words: *I don't know.*

THE STFU PARENT

You have heard of snowplow parents, the ones who jump in and clear away obstacles for their kids, and helicopter parents, who hover over their kids to make sure nothing ever goes wrong. Then come the tiger moms, who never leave their kids alone and who constantly badger them into doing their homework and practicing violin forty hours a day.

I propose we create a new kind of parent: the STFU parent.

No so very long ago, STFU parents were the norm. Parents were busy. They had things to do. Or, maybe they just wanted to sit in the living room drinking martinis and reading the paper. Nobody felt obliged to keep their kids busy or entertained, or to organize their schedule and keep their calendars full. The word *parenting*—as in, "to parent"—wasn't even in the dictionary until 1958, and it gained widespread use only in the 1970s. Before then, *parent* was a noun. It was something you *were*, not something you *did*.

But then parenting became a thing. Amazon has more than sixty thousand books on parenting. And now there is something even worse: *intensive parenting*. Piano lessons, swim lessons, soccer, karate, travel teams, Kumon, Khan Academy. In Boston, where I live, insane parents—my wife and I were once among them—send their kids to evening classes offered by the Russian School of Mathematics, aka Russian Math. It's too much. We all know it. But, as parents, we are afraid *not* to do it. The world has become more competitive. The gap between haves and have-nots is wider than ever before. We're terrified that our kids might not end up on the right side of that divide.

But in trying to help our kids, we're doing them a disservice. We're keeping them from developing important skills that they will need when they grow up—like how to solve problems, how to innovate and figure things out for themselves. We think we're arming them for adulthood when, in fact, we are undermining them and robbing them of the chance to grow and learn on their own.

We're also hurting their ability to be creative. Since 1990, the creativity of American kids has been plunging, to the point where, according to Kyung Hee Kim, a professor at the College of William and Mary, we have a "creativity crisis." We're grinding our kids in an education system that has become all about training them to perform well on standardized tests, a change that "has reduced children's playtime, which stifles imagination . . . leaving students little time to think or explore concepts in depth," Kim explains. Yet creativity is the most important skill kids need to develop for the decades ahead. It's the one thing that robots and machine learning can't replace.

THE UNBEARABLE POINTLESSNESS OF NAGGING

We might take a lesson from Indigenous cultures, in which, according to Michaeleen Doucleff, a science reporter at National Public Radio, parents have never lost touch with the hands-off approach, and their kids are better off for it. Our kids are growing in a much different kind of world and have different goals and expectations, but Doucleff believes we can learn from the Mayan families in Mexico, the Inuit families above the Arctic Circle, and the Hadzabe families in Tanzania with whom she has spent time. Their kids are happier and better behaved. The parents are calm, laid-back, and effective. They don't do any nagging, bribing, or yelling. They go out of their way not to tell their kids what to do, nor do they feed them constant praise.

"Next time your child misbehaves . . . turn your back and walk away," Doucleff advises in *Hunter, Gather, Parent: What Ancient Cultures Can Teach Us About the Lost Art of Raising Happy, Helpful Little Humans*. "Same goes for arguments and power struggles. If one starts to brew, close your mouth and walk away." Arguing with kids teaches them to enjoy arguing. Don't bargain. Don't raise your voice. "The next time you feel the urge to 'teach a lesson,' skip it. Pull out the tape and cover your mouth. The well-intended point will evaporate in the delivery and the child will carry away feelings residual of worthlessness," early-childhood educator Vicki Hoefle instructs in *Duct*

Tape Parenting, her manifesto and how-to guide for using undertalking as a parenting skill.

THE STFU TEACHER

According to Mary Dickinson Bird, an education professor at the University of Maine who trained future elementary school teachers, "Silence in the classroom helps students gain a deeper and more powerful understanding of a subject." Inspired by an old New England proverb, "Talk less, say more," Bird used to break her students into four-person teams and challenge them to solve a problem without talking. Each team was given a ten-liter tub filled with water and a bunch of random objects—corks, sticks, rubber bands, aluminum foil, metal washers, film canisters, marbles. The mix varied, but each team got a four-centimeter iron ball and had to create a way to carry the ball from one end of the tub to the other—from the island of Silencia to the island of Flotensia, as she put it. Teams bartered with one another for materials, spied on one another, and shared ideas, without speaking a word.

The game is frustrating but also fun, and "for students the exercise can be transforming," Bird wrote in *Science and Children*, a journal for educators. Shy kids get a chance to shine. Talkative kids get a chance to STFU and learn from others. Everyone learns about interpersonal skills and group dynamics.

Bird believed silence opens up new pathways to learning. Her exercise offers obvious potential benefits for teachers, managers, or parents trying to wrangle a bunch of whiny kids who are stuck inside on a rainy day. "By saying less, we have said a great deal indeed," Bird wrote.

LET YOUR KIDS PLAY

Parents can be either gardeners or carpenters, says Alison Gopnik, a psychologist at the University of California, Berkeley who specializes in children's development. Carpenters try to build their kids into the vision they have for them. Gardeners STFU and create the space for their kids to grow in whatever direction *they* want. You can probably guess which one is better.

Over the past three decades we have made the mistake of turning "parenting" into a job just like any other job, with goals, milestones, rules—and it's not working. We should just give kids space and let them play. Let them learn how to learn and how to be innovative and creative.

Fred Rogers became one of the greatest early-childhood educators by offering children "silence in a noisy world," his biographer wrote. He was a model for parents everywhere. As Mary McNamara wrote in the *Los Angeles Times*, "He paused almost as much as he spoke, often for a long time. But those pauses were not filled with empty air; they were filled with space."

Rogers didn't just teach kids; he taught parents, too. He modeled a form of calm interpersonal relating that brought out the best in the people around him. The same applies to us. When we STFU around our kids, we're modeling that behavior for them. Rogers used silence to devastating effect. One technique involved sitting with someone without speaking, sometimes for as long as sixty seconds.

In 1997, while receiving a Lifetime Achievement Award at the Emmy Awards, Rogers asked the audience to spend ten seconds in silence "to think of the people who have helped you become who you are, those who have cared for you, and wanted what is best for you in life." By the end of the ten seconds, people in the audience were weeping. You can watch the clip on YouTube; I dare you to do so without tearing up. I also dare you to do it with your kids. Silence, done well, can be devastating.

LET YOUR KIDS FAIL

It's painful to watch your kid struggle. It's unbearable. And they don't always figure things out on their own. Sometimes they fail. And you feel guilty, because you could have told them what to do or how to avoid the problem, but you didn't. You just sat there.

And then what do you do? Do you call the teacher and ask if your kid can have a do-over on the math test? Do you sit like a prison guard next to your kid to make sure he finishes his homework—or do the homework for him? Do you call the soccer coach and complain that your daughter isn't getting enough playing time?

No. What you do then is you continue to STFU.

This is really, really difficult. You know (or think you know) what your kids should be doing. Moreover, sometimes your kids *want* you to fix their problems for them. They ask you to do it. And you could do it. But you can't. Forcing yourself to STFU in these situations is one of the most challenging parts of being a parent. I hate it.

I have seen kids arrive at school with art projects that looked like they were done by a creative team on Madison Avenue. I have seen Cub Scouts bring cars to the pinewood derby that were built by grown men with engineering degrees. Those parents probably thought they were doing a great job. They were helping their kids be winners.

Resist the madness. Let your kid lose the race. Let them get an F on that test. Let them learn how it feels to be uncomfortable, afraid, worried, disappointed. It's terrifying to let this happen. But if we don't, we are not doing our kids any favors. We are robbing them of the chance to develop coping skills. We are making them feel powerless—and, in a way, we're treating them with disrespect.

According to neuropsychologist William Stixrud and educator Ned Johnson, authors of *The Self-Driven Child: The Science and Sense of Giving Your Kids More Control over Their Lives*, letting kids figure things out on their own—resisting the urge to correct them or help them and even being careful about how we praise them—makes them more confident and less likely to be crippled by anxiety and stress.

I am not suggesting we throw our kids to the wolves. According to to Diane Tavenner, cofounder and CEO of Summit Public Schools, a network of public schools in California and Washington, somewhere between doing their homework for them and sending them to an uninhabited island with a Swiss Army knife and a pack of matches, there is a middle ground where you can let your kids fail and learn from the experience. Tavenner encourages parents to let kids fail on small things, like homework: "Remember that the consequences of messing up one assignment or even a few are not life-altering." Think of yourself as a coach, she advises. Instead of providing answers, ask questions. The idea is to help kids build their skills so they can succeed on their own.

LET YOUR KIDS SUCCEED

The great thing about keeping quiet and giving your kids room to fail is that when they do succeed, the victory belongs completely to them. Michelle Obama says that's the best gift her parents gave her and her brother when they were growing up: "You made our successes and failures our own," Michelle told her mom, Marian Shields Robinson, when they had a conversation on the former First Lady's podcast.

It begins with small things. Marian never bugged the kids to get up on time and go to school. That was their job. Michelle Obama believes little things like that have a big pay-off later. "If you're looking for a child to be self-reliant when they're twenty-one or twenty-two, you have to make them practice that as young as five and seven years old," she said.

Marian, who lived in the White House with the Obamas and helped raise Malia and Sasha, says part of letting kids succeed is admitting that sometimes you don't know what to do, either. "Parents think they need to know all the answers. But nobody knows all the answers. I was very comfortable saying, 'I don't know.'"

Marian was a gardener, not a carpenter. She knew her daughter was strong-willed, and she figured, *Why try to change her?* "That was the gift that she gave me," the former First Lady once told an audience. "My parents saw this flame in me . . . and instead of doing what we often do to girls who are feisty, which is try to put that flame out, to douse it . . . they found a way to keep that flame lit, because they knew I'd need it later on. To have that flame lit in a girl means you have to value her voice and let her speak and learn how to use it."

Michelle Obama brought her mom's hands-off, let-them-try-and-fail approach to raising her daughters. "Being a mother is a master class in letting go," she told Meghan

Markle in an interview for British *Vogue*. "Motherhood has taught me that, most of the time, my job is to give them the space to explore and develop into the people they want to be. Not who I want them to be or who I wish I was at that age, but who they are, deep inside.

"Motherhood has also taught me that my job is not to bulldoze a path for them in an effort to eliminate all possible adversity. But instead, I need to be a safe and consistent place for them to land when they inevitably fail; and to show them, again and again, how to get up on their own."

LET YOUR KIDS BE BORED

Lin-Manuel Miranda swears by boredom. He says idle childhood afternoons spent daydreaming helped develop the imagination that produced *Hamilton*, one of the biggest Broadway hits of all time and winner of the Pulitzer Prize. "There is nothing better to spur creativity than a blank page or an empty bedroom," Miranda told *GQ*, adding that the key to parenting is to do a little less parenting. He might not put it this way, but I suspect Miranda is an STFU parent.

One tenet of STFU parenting is that it's not our job to entertain our kids. We don't owe them this. In fact, what we owe them is boredom, because boredom is good. A lot of new research shows that being bored helps kids be more creative and better able to self-regulate their emotions, for example. "I'm bored," they say. Great! The universe has handed you, and them, a gift. Resist the urge to fill their empty time. STFU and let them figure it out for themselves.

Boredom feels uncomfortable, but the bored brain develops an "internal stimulus" and goes looking for something to think about, says Teresa Belton, a professor of education and lifelong learning who studies the connections between boredom and creativity. Belton says kids need "stand-and-stare time," when they can just observe the world around them and let their brains drift into a daydreaming state.

Adults benefit from boredom, too. Psychology researchers found that people who performed a boring task before taking a test of creative thinking outperformed people in a control group. Albert Einstein was an inveterate loafer. He claimed that he got a lot of his best ideas while he was drifting around in a sailboat doing nothing. Steve Jobs spent a lot of time dawdling and putting things off. Aaron Sorkin gets so many great ideas in the shower that sometimes he takes six showers in a day.

That's insane. But so is the way we currently raise our kids. Do them a favor and STFU.

LET'S BRING BACK THE STIFF UPPER LIP

Say what you will about Queen Elizabeth, but the woman knew how to STFU. Her old-school, stiff-upper-lip restraint was her greatest strength. I'm sure it drove her crazy to be constantly cleaning up messes made by family members who lacked her self-discipline, but you never heard her complain. The Windsors are ridiculous people, and the monarchy is a ridiculous institution. The Queen seemed to know this but also to realize that the only way to keep the charade from falling apart was for her to STFU, stay out of trouble, and never let anyone know what she was thinking. For all we know, the Queen cared about nothing other than corgis and horses.

And that's great. That's fantastic. We should all learn

from her. The world doesn't need to know how we feel about everything—or anything. We're told that it's bad to repress our feelings, but is it? Keeping things to yourself seems better than spewing your problems and opinions on everyone around you. As the Queen might have said, STFU and carry on.

Her son King Charles once complained to a biographer that the Queen wasn't a very good mother, that she was cold and uncaring, and that during his early years, she left him in the care of nannies while she was traveling around the world on royal duties. He may have been right about his mother's lack of affection for him. As Tina Brown writes in *The Palace Papers*, "The sorry truth was that Charles, in his material character, just wasn't the kind of person the Queen admired." Who could blame her? As with everything else, the Queen's response to Charles's bleating about her parenting skills was perfect: she said nothing.

Charles has been derided in the British press as a "prat," a "twit," and an "idiot," who has bombarded members of Parliament with letters lobbying for causes ranging from climate change to cattle farming, from the war in Iraq to how teachers should run their classrooms, from herbal medicines to huts in Antarctica and the fate of the endangered Patagonian toothfish. His messy personal life has caused endless problems for the family. First was the messy marriage to Diana, followed by the even messier divorce, and the cringe-inducing "sexy" phone calls with Camilla, his future wife. At each turn, his mother let him fail, then rushed in and made things right for him.

When Charles and Diana separated, the Queen zipped her lips for a few years—until Diana went on the BBC with journalist Martin Bashir and blubbered about Charles and his family. Containing her rage, the Queen sent a messenger to Diana's door with a hand-carried letter that read, in essence, *You're done.* Then she issued a terse public statement announcing that Charles and Diana would be getting divorced. That was it. No interviews. No crying on *Dr. Phil* about how Diana had hurt her feelings. The Queen did her job and STFU about it.

When Diana died, the Queen seemed inclined to stick with her policy of not saying anything, but then her pathetic subjects started moaning that their monarch wasn't enough of a soppy mess like them. To avert a crisis, she gave an emotionless three-minute live address on the BBC in which she performed her duty—say something nice about Diana, be polite, pretend to feel something but not too much, blah, blah, blah.

At Diana's funeral, the Queen bowed her head before Diana's coffin, which was a big deal and a breach of protocol—the monarch does not bow to other people—but also a brilliant PR move that restored support for the royal family. This was STFU. Without speaking a word, the Queen said everything. Maybe she hated having to bow. Or maybe she really meant it. We'll never know—because the Queen, unlike everyone else around her, was savvy enough to remain an enigma, "an empty mirror for the nation to gaze upon itself," as Brown puts it.

After mopping up after Charles and Diana, the Queen was given the chore of saving the monarchy from her son Andrew, who is even worse than his brother. Andrew scandalized the family with a made-for-the-tabloids marriage and divorce. Not satisfied to end there, he then caused an even more sordid mess because of his friendship with the pedophile Jeffrey Epstein and a lawsuit from an Epstein victim who alleged that Andrew had sexually abused her when she was a minor. The Queen settled the lawsuit, stripped Andrew of his titles and responsibilities, and stuck him in a box for the rest of his life. Problem solved. Never a word about it in public.

When the Queen's self-indulgent grandson Harry quit the family to make a living by getting psychotherapy in public, moaning to Oprah about his lousy childhood, she stripped him and his wife, Meghan Markle, of the right to call themselves "royal"—a punishment made more powerful by the silence that surrounded it. Harry callously aired his complaints while his grandfather lay dying in the hospital. He would have done better to heed his grandfather's old-school advice: "Give TV interviews by all means. But don't talk about yourself."

The Queen's emotional restraint might have had some drawbacks, but it's better than the narcissism and lack of manners shown by others in the family, says Martin Francis, a British historian, who criticized Prince William for saying that "The days of the 'stiff upper lip' have to end." Do they? Really? Surely you can talk to a shrink about your problems in private. Going on TV to tell the world about them is not therapeutic; it's selfish. Says Martin, "The stiff upper lip . . . still has a great deal to recommend it."

Amen to that.

HAPPY FINNS

In 2022, Finland was named the happiest country in the world for the fifth year in a row. There are probably lots of reasons for this, but the biggest is that Finns know how to STFU. Finns are among the most quiet, reserved people in the world. They are extreme undertalkers. Unlike Americans, who can't stand even a few seconds of silence, Finns are perfectly content to sit together without speaking. "Silence is gold, talking is silver" is a Finnish proverb. While Americans put individual needs and accomplishments above all else, Finns value harmony and balance.

When the Covid-19 lockdowns came, and Finns were required to stay two meters apart, the joke in Finland was "Why can't we stick to our usual four meters?" Another Finnish joke: "How do you know when a Finn likes you? When they stare at your shoes instead of their own." Finland is so quiet that its tourism board once created an entire campaign around the idea it called "silence travel," which was aimed especially at tourists from China. "Looking for a place so quiet that you can hear yourself think? Allow us to introduce the quiet forests, idyllic villages, ancient holy sites, and national parks of Finnish Lapland."

Kimi Räikkönen, a champion Formula One driver from Finland, was famous for his skills on the track but even more so for saying almost nothing off the track. When he retired, a teammate said, "I will miss the silence." Later, Räikkönen said he might consent to making a movie about his career, but "only a silent one."

Finland has one of the best education systems in the world—way better than the American system—and it is a model of STFU restraint. No pressure. No standardized tests. Kids start school at a later age, have shorter school days, and spend a lot of time playing. Yet when Finnish kids are measured in academic prowess against kids from other countries, they're always near the top, and they out-perform American kids by a huge margin.

Finnish parents are what I call STFU parents and what Alison Gopnik would describe as gardeners rather than carpenters. Their approach to raising kids looks nothing like ours. There are no helicopter parents or tiger moms. Finns give their kids hours of playtime every day, let them learn at their own pace, and place a high value on their developing independence, self-reliance, manners, and caring about others. Finnish kids come home, make lunch, and do their homework on their own. Finnish families build backyard play huts called *leikimokki* in which kids play with their friends and even sleep in summer.

Finns should not be happy people. The weather is miserable in Finland. In winter, they get only a few hours of daylight, and their winter lasts one hundred days in the south, around Helsinki, and two hundred days in the north. Somehow, they manage to be happy anyway, and I suspect it's because they know how to STFU and stay out of one another's hair. Finns aren't antisocial. They love hanging out naked in a sauna with friends. They just don't like to make small talk. And they manage to communicate without using words.

JAPAN: QUIET PARENTING

In Japan, the art of communicating without speaking is called *haragei*, or "belly talk." It means the ability to express an opinion or convey an idea without saying anything out loud, instead using facial expressions, shrugs, eye movement, and other nonverbal cues. You're talking from your belly rather than with your mouth. This works in Japan, which is considered a "high-context" culture, one where people understand one another and don't need to be explicit—a collectivist society. On average, Japanese conversations contain twice as much silence as the conversations of Americans.

Japanese also have a concept called *ishin-denshin*, which can be translated as "telepathy," meaning the ability to understand someone else without their speaking. Then there's *sontaku*, what we would call "reading between the lines." For the Japanese, these are subtle, artful, and efficient ways of communicating. Silence doesn't freak them out the way it freaks out Americans. Japanese consider silence a sign of respect. Being silent in conversation means you're thinking about what the other person has just said. Silence is also a sign of intelligence: in Japan, people who speak plainly or talk too much are seen as common, childish, dumb.

Silence plays a big role in parenting in Japan and helps explain why the Japanese are so much better at it than we are. Westerners who move to Japan with their kids are stunned to see two-year-olds sitting calmly and quietly in restaurants and public places. That's because their parents are masters of quiet parenting who have taught their children restraint, self-discipline, and manners by modeling these behaviors for them.

When American novelist Kate Lewis moved to Japan with her young daughter and toddler son, she was embarrassed by the contrast between her own wild, noisy American kids and their Japanese counterparts. She found that Japanese parents take a different approach to discipline, which they call *shitsuke*, which translates as "training" or "upbringing." *Shitsuke* is a quiet approach. Instead of

yelling at the kid in the playground or at the mall—think
of how many times you've seen that happen or even done it
yourself—Japanese parents wait and have a quiet talk with
their kids in private. "I began noticing this everywhere—
parents crouched behind pillars in train stations, at the edges
of parks, having quiet conversations," Lewis explained in
an article for *Savvy Tokyo*.

There's a catch, however. Unlike those happy Finns,
Japan usually ranks near the bottom in annual surveys that
rank happiness. In a 2019 survey of twenty-nine countries,
Japan ranked twenty-third. In the 2020 edition of the United
Nations' annual World Happiness Report, Japan ranked
sixty-second. But that's probably because its citizens' defi-
nition of happiness is not the one that Western pollsters are
looking for. Westerners define happiness as feeling excited,
scoring big wins, achieving great things. The Japanese value
quieter things.

Also, Japan has the highest longevity in the world. Diet
and genetics contribute to that, but so does *ikigai*, a word
that translates as "the happiness of always being busy" but
means having a purposeful, meaningful life. *Ikigai* has
become kind of a cottage industry in the West—you'll find
lots of books and TED Talks about it.

On the island of Okinawa, a village called Ogimi has
the highest percentage of one-hundred-year-olds of any
place on earth—and the *ikigai* is off the charts, according
to Héctor García and Francesc Miralles, who visited Ogimi
and interviewed the oldsters. *Ikigai* has a lot in common
with the "meaningful, substantive conversations" that University of Arizona psychologist Matthias Mehl found to
be the key to better mental health and a stronger immune

system. Talk less, listen more, avoid small talk, make real connections. It's a pretty simple recipe.

STFU is selfless. It brings out the best in the people around you. Listening to someone, putting all your attention on them instead of on yourself, does magic. Winston Churchill's mother, Jennie Jerome, once contrasted the experience of having dinner with two big-shot British politicians, William Gladstone and Benjamin Disraeli: "When I left the dining room after sitting next to Gladstone, I thought he was the cleverest man in England. But when I sat next to Disraeli, I left feeling that I was the cleverest woman."

Imagine having that effect on everyone in your life. Imagine making your kids happier, more independent, better able to succeed. Imagine unlocking their creativity so that they can solve the world's most challenging problems. Imagine being able to bring out the best in your friends and relatives or even the random strangers you meet in your day-to-day life. Then imagine that goodness radiating outward, as our kids, friends, and relatives do the same for the people in their lives. There is more to STFU than just talking less and getting more for yourself. If enough of us learned to STFU, we could make the world a little bit better for all of us.

8

STFU IN LOVE

My wife and I spent years going to marriage counselors. There was the gruff middle-aged guy who charged a fortune and made us sit side by side on a couch and told me I should do more of the cooking. There was the sweet, soft-spoken older guy who wore cardigan sweaters and Harris tweed jackets and said we should go on dates and romantic weekends. There was the sixtysomething woman who wore dangly earrings and socks with sandals and made us do breathing exercises, followed by another sixtysomething woman with dangly earrings and socks with sandals, who told us, flat out, to quit going to counseling and just break up already.

So, we did. This is how I found myself sitting alone in a rented house in the early days of the Covid-19 lockdown realizing that pretty much every bad thing that had ever happened to me, including losing my family, could have been avoided if only I had been able to STFU. This was the moment when I started trying to figure out how to do it.

Years of talking to counselors had done nothing for us. In fact, the more we talked, the worse things got. What we really needed to do was talk less, to heed the advice of the late Supreme Court justice Ruth Bader Ginsburg and try to "be a little deaf." Thanks to that policy, RBG and her husband, Martin, enjoyed a marriage that most of us only dream about, the kind where you grow old together and never fall out of love. It was "fifty-six years of a marital partnership nonpareil," as RBG described it.

In addition to being a little deaf, it helps to be a little bit mute. But I had no Mute button. I could never resist saying what I was thinking. But now, alone, separated from my wife and kids, I set myself to the task of developing one. I clung to a piece of advice that my shrink repeated to me like a mantra: "You can always say nothing." When someone hurts your feelings, you don't have to respond. In fact, you literally never have to open your mouth and speak, in any situation. An environmentalist named John Francis gave up speaking for seventeen years and still managed to complete a PhD and become a UN Goodwill Ambassador. I'm not suggesting we should go that far; I'm just saying it's possible.

I began working on my daily STFU practice wherever and whenever I could. In a demonstration of how crazy for therapy our culture has become, someone suggested that my wife and I speak to yet another marriage counselor—not to salvage the relationship, but to learn how to manage our breakup. But the last thing we needed was more talk therapy. What we needed was non-talk therapy.

We still had to interact with each other because of the kids, but we tried to do this quietly. To be sure, we still sometimes exchanged angry text messages and had phone calls that ended with one of us hanging up on the other. But we tried to follow a second piece of advice from RBG:

"When a thoughtless or unkind word is spoken, best tune out. Reacting in anger or annoyance will not advance one's ability to persuade."

Shrinks say couples need to learn how to have a fight. I say we would be better off learning how *not* to fight in the first place, as RBG advised. My wife and I didn't hash things out or relitigate old arguments. We didn't talk about each other's flaws. We let things go. And I began to develop a Mute button. With some trepidation, we began spending time alone together without saying very much. This was a different kind of silent treatment, not the one we used to inflict on each other when we were angry. We took our dog for walks in the woods. We went out for dinner.

Before walking into the restaurant to meet her, I would sit in my car, take deep breaths, and run through my STFU checklist. Over dinner, I listened instead of talking, asked questions instead of delivering Danalogues, and let pauses hang in the conversation. I challenged myself to spend an entire meal saying only things that mirrored what she said, having no agenda of my own, saying things like "Huh," or "That's interesting."

We did not try to get all lovey-dovey or rekindle the passion of our early days and fall back in love. Sometimes we just sat and said nothing. In my pre-STFU days, this would have driven me up the wall. But now, instead of rushing to fill the void, I had learned to sit with that anxious feeling until it dissipated. Over time, the anxiety became easier to contain. After several months, we set aside our differences and got back together. I can't promise that non-talk therapy will work for you. But being "a little deaf" worked for RBG and her husband, and it worked for us, too. It's worth a try.

WILL YOU PLEASE BE QUIET, PLEASE?

Our noisy culture believes in talking. We talk things out. We talk things over. We talk things through. And how's that working out for us? Nearly half of married couples go to couples counseling, and yet half of first marriages fail. Second and third marriages have even higher failure rates. Twenty-five percent of couples who go to therapy end up *worse* than they were before. This is success?

Part of the problem is that working with couples is difficult, and most therapists receive no special training in how to do it, according to William Doherty, a psychologist at the University of Minnesota: "From a consumer's point of view, going in for couples therapy is like having your broken leg set by a doctor who skipped orthopedics in medical school," he wrote, in an article titled "How Therapy Can Be Hazardous to Your Marital Health." But the bigger problem might be simply that having it out with each other in front of a shrink is a bad idea to begin with. Maybe those fifty-minute kvetch sessions do nothing but reinforce the bad habits you've already developed.

Researchers at the University of Groningen in the Netherlands found that couples become closer when they spend time together in silence. Psychologist Suzanne Phillips, who works with couples recovering from trauma, espouses the power of "Just Being There," based on the notion that focusing on nonverbal cues connects people at a level beyond their conscious awareness. She advises clients to carve out time to spend with each other in silence, to do things like meditating together, walking in nature, or taking car rides without speaking. "A couple's ability to have separate silence while remaining bonded reflects their independence as well as their bond," she suggests.

This may explain why the hours that my wife and I spent engaging in STFU therapy accomplished what years of expensive talk therapy never could: we got back together. Since then, I have continued to focus on STFU at home, and it has made all the difference.

STFU AND FALL IN LOVE

In 1967, psychologist Arthur Aron developed a magic spell that can make two strangers fall in love. To invoke the spell, you ask each other thirty-six questions that grow more and more personal. Then comes the closer: After finishing the questions, you stare into each other's eyes for four minutes *without speaking*—and the spell is sealed. You're in love.

Aron, a professor at the State University of New York at Stony Brook, does not claim this to be a foolproof method that will work with anyone. You need to have some things in common and some basic attraction to each other. But if you do, answering the questions and staring at each other "could be the straw that breaks the camel's back," Aron has said, adding that this might be the most important thing you will ever do. "Love is central to human life. Relationship quality is the biggest predictor of human happiness, more than wealth or success. And it's a huge predictor of health. How long we'll live is predicted more strongly by your relationship quality than by smoking or obesity."

Aron's method works so well that other researchers

use it in experiments, calling it the "relationship closeness induction task." Mandy Len Catron, a university writing teacher, used the Aron exercise with an acquaintance and ended up in a relationship with him, an experience she described in the *New York Times* and later turned into a book, *How to Fall in Love with Anyone.* Catron and her friend sat in a bar and, over a few beers, worked through Aron's questions. As she tells it, moving through the questions made the two friends more and more vulnerable, and in a few hours they developed a degree of closeness that might have taken months to develop under ordinary circumstances. After finishing the questions, they stood on a bridge gazing into each other's eyes for four minutes, which Catron describes in her *New York Times* article as "one of the most thrilling and terrifying experiences of my life." "The real crux of the moment was not just that I was really seeing someone, but that I was seeing someone really seeing me." It worked. They fell in love and began a relationship.

It's hard to say which is more important, the questions or the four minutes of silence. Probably neither would work without the other. But the four-minute silent gaze has a lot of power on its own. A few years ago, during the refugee crisis in Europe, Amnesty International conducted an experiment where refugees sat across from Europeans and made silent eye contact for four minutes. The goal was to help people on different sides of a contentious issue find empathy with one another. The results, shown in a five-minute video, brought me to tears. People smiled. Some wept. Or laughed. Or hugged. "Four minutes of eye contact brings people closer to each other better than everything else," the organizers declared.

The power of the exercise arises not just from eye contact, but from the silence. It's another example of how the
absence of words can convey more than words. The partners did talk to each other after the four-minute exercise,
and their conversations were intense. One man and woman
seemed to have fallen in love already and to be heading
toward a relationship. Their four minutes of silence were
not four minutes of emptiness. This was active silence.
They were communicating and building a connection that
was deeper and stronger than what they could have done by
talking. Silence does not mean an absence of communication; it can be loaded with meaning. The French mime Mar-
cel Marceau once described it this way: "Music and silence
combine strongly because music is done with silence, and
silence is full of music."

THE 60–40 RULE

Michael Beatty, the communication professor who figured out the cause of talkaholism, teaches a course at the
University of Miami called Romantic Communication—
basically, the role of verbal and nonverbal communication
in relationships. Beatty explains dopamine and serotonin,
but the most important thing he teaches, as far as his students are concerned, is how to communicate on a first date
if you hope to get a second one. His course is always oversubscribed.

Beatty says the biggest thing is balance, which he describes
as the 60–40 Rule. "For a date to be successful, neither person should speak more than sixty percent of the time or less
than forty percent. If you do all the talking, the other person is overwhelmed. But if you sit there and say nothing, too

much burden falls on the other person. Either way it's not going to work," he told me.

It appears that when it comes to dating, talkaholics are pretty much doomed, or at least operating from an extreme disadvantage. Undertalkers, for their part, do better at attracting the opposite sex, perhaps because their under-talking exudes confidence. Beatty uses James Bond as an example. No matter who plays the role, whether Sean Connery or Daniel Craig, Bond is always an undertalker. "Short answers are better than long answers, and one word is ideal. But it's not just that Bond gives short answers, it's the facial expression plus the short answer," Beatty said. "Bond rarely shows his teeth." Beatty says it's a primate thing. Showing one's teeth is a sign of submission. "Tom Cruise is all teeth, which is why women don't see him as an alpha. They see him as a child."

But what about the 60–40 Rule? I asked. James Bond talks a lot less than 40 percent, yet women can't resist him. How does he get away with it?

Beatty offers a simple explanation: "He's James Bond. You're not."

HOW TO TALK GOODER

Another way to raise your chances of getting a second date: ask questions. Harvard Business School professor Alison Wood Brooks studies the art of conversation in business contexts, but one of her experiments involved studying speed daters. Brooks teaches a course called How to Talk Gooder and promotes a conversational practice she calls "TALK," short for "Topic selection, Asking questions, Levity, and Kindness." Being able to "talk gooder" can help

MBA students claw their way to the top of the corporate ladder. But Brooks's methods can help you find a romantic partner, too.

Brooks and a few other Harvard researchers studied the results of a speed-dating experiment where graduate students were put into an auditorium and zipped through twenty four-minute speed dates. Afterward, the speed daters were asked whether they would go on a second date with each of the people they met. The people who asked the most questions in their four-minute dates got more second date offers. "In fact, asking just one more question on each date meant that participants persuaded one additional person (over the course of 20 dates) to go out with them again," Woods explained in a *Harvard Business Review* article.

In another study, Harvard researchers arranged fifteen-minute online conversations for test subjects, instructing some to ask nine or more questions and others to ask no more than four questions. Again, the people who asked more questions were better liked by their conversation partners.

There are limits, however. Asking too many questions can backfire, as your partner may feel overwhelmed by the barrage. Striking the right balance—mastering the STFU skills of asking and listening—could be key to finding the person of your dreams.

THE 7–38–55 RULE

Another thing to remember when you're talking to a partner is that very little of your meaning is conveyed by the words you speak—only about 7 percent, according to research done a half century ago by Albert Mehrabian, a psychologist at the University of California, Los Angeles. The rest is being communicated by your tone of voice and body language—38 percent and 55 percent, respectively, according to Mehrabian's 7–38–55 Rule.

Mehrabian explained the 7–38–55 Rule in his 1971 book, *Silent Messages*, which has been used by everyone from business coaches to FBI hostage negotiators like Chris Voss. Voss suggests you can gain an edge by reading nonverbal cues and looking for inconsistencies or contradictions between what's being said and what is being conveyed by body language—mixed messages, in other words.

Mehrabian arrived at his results by having students listen to recordings of words like *honey, maybe,* and *brute* spoken in three different tones—"liking," "neutral," and "disliking"—while looking at photos meant to convey the same three emotional states. He found that visual images did a better job of conveying meaning.

Mehrabian's research methods have been criticized, and Mehrabian himself has claimed at times that his results were being misunderstood and taken out of context. You can quibble with the numbers—maybe the split should be 10–20–70, or 30–20–50—but it's hard to dismiss the general idea that nonverbal cues convey more than actual spoken words.

The 7–38–55 principle gives you a powerful tool for communicating with a partner, both for understanding what your partner is really trying to tell you, or trying to hide, and for making sure you are communicating clearly. If your partner uses more words than necessary or speaks more emphatically than usual when they try to explain where they were last night, some detective work may be in order. Figuring this out requires you to adopt the STFU discipline and let your partner do most of the talking. Sit back, ask questions, let long pauses hang, and, most important, observe. Watch their body language. Listen to the tone of their voice. Keep your tone measured and in control. Be open and direct with your body language. Don't grill. Don't argue or interrogate. The less you talk, the more you will learn.

In less contentious situations—when you're in an ordinary conversation, say, or having a heart-to-heart about the relationship and your feelings—keep the 7–38–55 Rule front and center. Your spoken words matter, but not as much as you think, and you don't need a lot of them. Focus instead on the tone of your delivery. If you come across as strident or overly assertive, you will throw up obstacles that make it less likely for your partner to understand what you're saying. Think about your body language. Maintain eye contact and a neutral facial expression. Keep an open posture.

BEWARE THE FOUR HORSEMEN

The way you talk is so connected to the success of a relationship that shrinks can tell just by listening to your conversation whether you will end up getting divorced. John Gottman, a psychologist at the University of Washington, developed a method that could predict with nearly 90 percent accuracy whether a newlywed couple would end up getting divorced based on the way they talked to each other.

His work began with a study in which he interviewed fifty-two married couples and observed their behavior as they answered questions about the history of their relationship. Using those conversations, Gottman predicted which couples he believed would break up. When he checked in three years later, his predictions were nearly perfect.

Once Gottman could predict that people would break up by studying the way they communicated with each other, he could teach couples how to "talk gooder" so that they would not get divorced, or would at least have a better chance of staying together. This became the Gottman Method of Marital Therapy, which grew into the Gottman Institute. Gottman has authored or coauthored forty books. There's an entire industry built around his ideas, and a lot of advice involves various ways of learning how to STFU.

Among couples who end up getting divorced, Gottman identified four negative ways of interacting, which he called the "Four Horsemen": criticism, contempt, defensiveness, and stonewalling. Contempt is the worst one and evolves from the other three. Gottman talks about "flooding," the feeling of being overwhelmed by your partner's contempt or criticism.

Gottman believes in talk therapy, and he's firmly in the "learn how to have a fight" camp. Though I'm not a fan of "talking it out," there are aspects of Gottman's approach that make sense, like the notion that when you start feeling flooded, you should STFU and bail out.

Take a twenty-minute break. Do something that makes you feel calm. Go for a walk. Taking time to cool down and self-soothe might convince you that you don't need to have this conversation at all. But if you want to resume it, you will be in a better state of mind to do it calmly. Also, once you are able to soothe yourself, you will be better able to soothe your partner. If your partner returns the favor, you will end up developing a Soothe-a-Rama virtuous circle.

Gottman talks about "harsh startups" and "soft start-ups" to describe the way a conversation begins. Start a conversation with sarcasm or negativity, and things are not going to go well. Going in soft means using some STFU strategies, like keeping your voice low, leaving pauses, speaking slowly and with intention, using few words, and trying to listen.

Other Gottman advice: Let things go. You can't resolve everything, so why bother? Some stuff is just there, and it's going to stay there. Maybe you are married to a person who keeps all the kitchen tools (blender, mixer, Crock-Pot, rice maker, toaster, kettle, cutting boards) on the kitchen counter at all times, even though some are rarely used and they make your tiny kitchen look cluttered, and clutter drives you crazy, and when you put these things away, your partner takes them out and puts them back on the counter. (Ask me where I got this example.) This is a problem you are not going to solve. Do you want to break up over it?

Learn how to compromise, and realize what compromise means: "Compromise is not one person changing. It's about negotiating and discovering ways to accommodate each other. Compromise is impossible unless you accept your partner's flaws," the Gottman Institute advises.

Train yourself to ignore the clutter in your kitchen. Learn to be a little bit blind as well as a little deaf. Remind yourself to STFU.

TEACH YOURSELF TO STOP

Jon Kabat-Zinn got a PhD in molecular biology at the Massachusetts Institute of Technology, but then studied

Buddhism and ended up becoming a mindfulness professor and founder of the Stress Reduction Clinic at the University of Massachusetts Medical School. Kabat-Zinn developed a skill called "STOP" that has become widely used in the practice of cognitive behavioral therapy and works great in relationships. It can help you STFU when you're about to say something that will get you in trouble or that you will later regret.

STOP stands for:

- *Stop*: Pause what you're doing; whatever you're about to say, don't say it.

- *Take a breath*: Breathing anchors you emotionally.

- *Observe*: What is happening inside you? How are you feeling physically, in your body? Why are you feeling this way?

- *Proceed*: If you still think it is important or necessary to speak, do it with intention and mindfulness. But maybe you can let go of it and leave that thought unsaid.

This little exercise is ridiculously simple, but devilishly difficult. It requires discipline, and practice, to learn how to hit the brakes. But in the year and a half since my wife and I got back together, it has saved me more times than I'd like to admit.

THE TRAFFIC LIGHT RULE

According to Marty Nemko, a psychologist, career coach, and NPR host, people stop paying attention to you after only thirty seconds. So, when you're having coffee with that person you just matched with on Tinder, it's not enough to stick to the 60–40 Rule and balance out the talking between the two of you. You also need to break up your comments into smaller chunks.

Toward this end, Nemko developed the Traffic Light Rule. For the first thirty seconds, you have a green light and can talk away. But at the thirty-second mark, the light turns yellow. Your partner's attention has started to drift or, worse, they might be hoping you will wrap things up. You can go through the yellow light—but proceed with caution, and only after reading the other person's facial expression and body language. If their eyes are glazing over, put the ball in their court.

At the one-minute mark, you've hit a red light. Your Tinder date has stopped hearing what you're saying and is instead checking out someone else in the back of the café. Go on much longer, and they will take out their phone and open their Tinder app to see who else they've matched with.

"There are rare times you should 'run a red light': when your listener is obviously fully engaged," Nemko advises. "But usually, when an utterance exceeds one minute, with each passing second, you increase the risk of boring your listener and having them think of you as a chatterbox, windbag, or blowhard."

Nemko suggests stopping at the thirty-second mark to see if your partner wants to hear more. If they do, they will ask. But they rarely do. If you need to explain something that takes more than a minute, Nemko recommends breaking it into thirty-second sections and stopping at the end of each section to ask a question. "Is this making sense? What do you think?"

The thirty-second tune-out has a scientific explanation, which has to do with neurophysiology and hormones, Nemko's friend, colleague, and fellow Traffic Light Rule endorser Mark Goulston says. Goulston, a psychiatrist and the author of *Just Listen: Discover the Secret to Getting Through to Absolutely Anyone*, says that when you begin talking, your brain is bathing in dopamine, the feel-good hormone. And you don't want that to stop. The result is what Goulston calls momentum deafness: "When you're on a roll, smoke gets in your ears" is how he puts it.

The problem is that while you are generating dopamine, you're causing the other person to produce cortisol, the feel-bad, fight-or-flight hormone, which makes them feel stressed out and resentful. Think about how you feel when someone goes on too long in a conversation. You start feeling anxious, even claustrophobic. You're dying to escape. More important, pay attention to how quickly you start to get this feeling. As Nemko says, this probably happens within thirty seconds, and certainly in less than a minute. The challenge is that time is a funny thing when you're talking. Thirty seconds feels like three seconds when you're talking but three minutes when you're listening.

Pro tip: practice with a smartwatch. Set a timer to buzz your wrist when you've hit thirty seconds or sixty seconds. Begin by doing this on phone calls or while Zooming, so the other person can't see you looking at your phone. But you can do this in person without drawing much attention to yourself, with the discreet push of a button. After a while, you will know how long thirty or sixty seconds feels, and you won't need a timer. You can also use a timer to see how long it takes for you to start feeling annoyed when someone else is talking. You can even quantify your level of annoyance by tracking your heart rate.

Nemko admits that it's hard to keep things short, but he emphasizes that abiding by the Traffic Light Rule is not entirely about being generous or polite. You're not helping the other person; you're helping yourself: "You'll get more of what you want if you trade in your talk-talk-talk self for someone who truly listens as much as he or she talks."

For what it's worth, the Traffic Light Rule applies on Tinder profiles, too. Tinder founder Sean Rad's advice on how to craft the perfect profile: "Keep it short and sweet," he told *GQ*. "No one starts swiping looking for a novel. We have a 500-character limit for a reason."

Those five hundred characters work out to a little bit more than one hundred words. It takes a bit over twenty seconds to read them. It might be even better to stay well under that five-hundred-character limit. The idea is to get someone interested while holding something back so that there's a reason to have a conversation IRL. When you do have that conversation, remember the Traffic Light Rule and STFU.

9

STFU IS POWER

If you work at Condé Nast and you email Anna Wintour to complain about a colleague, the editor of *Vogue* and content chief for all Condé Nast magazines will pull a savage move: instead of replying, she sends your email to the person you complained about. I'm guessing nobody ever makes this mistake twice. Also, Wintour never puts a subject line on an email. Why waste time?

Amazon founder Jeff Bezos employs the "Bezos Question Mark Method." If someone inside or outside the company emails him with a complaint, he forwards the message to the person responsible, adding just a single character: "?" People live in fear of getting a question mark email from their notoriously demanding boss.

This is quiet power. Bezos and Wintour don't need to raise their voices. They don't need to speak at all. All they do is click—and people tremble. It helps that Bezos and Wintour are already powerful and scary. Both practice the reign-of-terror method of management and have a superhuman ability to make people cry. Both also cultivate the look of Bond villains. Wintour is British, wears oversize sunglasses, and may or may not have a second row of tiny razor-sharp teeth. Her cruelty and ruthlessness are legendary. Same goes for Bezos, who insults top executives and, despite having a net worth of more than one hundred billion dollars, reportedly has told employees that they should pay *him* to work at Amazon. Once a nebbishy dweeb, Bezos, since becoming a billionaire, has transformed himself into Doctor Evil: shaved head, superyachts, phallic spaceships, Nehru jackets.

Even at the beginning of her career, working entry-level jobs in her early twenties, Wintour stood out by saying almost nothing, a lot like her father, a powerful newspaper editor in London. At dinner, she sat in silence. "Anna's power in those days, such as it was as a fashion assistant, lay in her silence," an acquaintance recalled to Amy Odell, author of *Anna: The Biography*. Another marveled at Wintour's "Cheshire-cat silence. You knew there was a lot going on in her head. But she just wasn't sharing it." On a walk to a meeting, Wintour spoke not a word, prompting a colleague to ask, "Don't you chat?" Wintour: "I chat to my friends."

Bezos and Wintour are using silence not to *obtain* power—they already have all they need—but to *maintain* it. They understand something important: Silence is power, and power is silence. Talking squanders power. It's as if you start with a fully charged battery, and every word you use drains the juice. "Powerful people impress and intimidate by saying less," Robert Greene declares in *The 48 Laws of Power*, his primer on how to obtain power and wield it to your advantage. "The more you say, the more common you appear." The third of Greene's forty-eight laws: "Conceal your intentions." The fourth: "Always say less than necessary."

The less you say, the more mysterious you become, and mystery is powerful. Andy Warhol refused to explain his paintings and drove interviewers crazy by giving weird, noncommittal answers. He once went on *The Merv Griffin Show* and communicated with nods and whispers, saying only yes and no. You couldn't look away. "I learned that you actually have more power when you shut up," Warhol said.

Powerful people always talk less than the people around them. That's why there's no such thing as the strong, talkative type. Overtalkers are perceived as weak, incompetent, and unsure of themselves, while undertalkers come across as strong, mysterious, and confident. Think of the difference between Clint Eastwood as Dirty Harry and Jim Carrey as Ace Ventura. They're both detectives, but one is a cool badass, and the other is a clown. One has relationships with women, and the other lives with a monkey named Spike.

Even if you do not aspire to be a San Francisco detective who takes the law into his own hands while wielding the most powerful handgun in the world, or a tyrannical fashion magazine editor who intimidates underlings, or a tech billionaire who rides rockets into space, you need power. Power is how we survive. It's how we exert control over the world around us, in everything from little, day-to-day things to momentous, life-changing decisions. Our brains crave the feeling of being in control and dread the feeling of being helpless or powerless. That feeling is what drove so many people bonkers during the Covid-19 lockdowns.

Yet, without even realizing it, most of us constantly squander our power in ways big and small. Think back to any major screwup in your life—the kind of thing that makes you cringe when you think about it, something you regret or wish you could do over—and usually, in one way or another, the trouble began because you squandered power. You lost control. You gave up an advantage. You failed to STFU.

Louis XIV was by nature an overtalking windbag, but he trained himself to STFU so that he could exert power over the people around him. By remaining silent and letting everyone else talk, Louis learned everything about them, while they never had any idea what he was thinking. "Louis's silence kept those around him terrified and under his thumb. It was one of the foundations of his power," Greene writes.

CONCISION CONVEYS POWER

Here is the secret to powerful communication: the fewer words you use, the more impact each one has. President John F. Kennedy's speech at the Berlin Wall—the "Ich bin ein Berliner" speech—took less than ten minutes. Franklin Delano Roosevelt's "Day of Infamy" speech ran six and a half. Winston Churchill's "Never Give In" speech ran four. Surely you can whip through your morning stand-up meeting in less time than it took those leaders to rouse nations.

A good place to start is email. Powerful people don't have time to waste writing long emails. The same rule applies to email as to meetings: keep them small and short. The fewer emails you send, and the fewer words you use, the more powerful you will appear to be.

Marketing guru Guy Kawasaki says the perfect email contains five sentences. It's okay to use fewer, but never use more. Writing long emails wrecks your productivity and burdens the recipient. The average worker spends 28 percent of their day reading email, according to McKinsey. Why add to that ocean of dreck?

Former *New Yorker* editor Tina Brown was almost as terrifying as Anna Wintour. At one time, the two competed to see who could be the meanest meanie inside Condé Nast, a place so mean that people called it "Condé Nasty." Like Wintour, Brown was skilled in the art of power messaging. Part of her legend among staffers was a memorable (and possibly apocryphal) text message she sent to an editor inquiring about an author named Nathaniel Fick. Her simple question: "Who fuck fick?"

Short emails show people you're busy and that you know what you're talking about. Long, rambling emails create the impression that you don't know what you're doing, have not thought things through enough, and don't respect other people's time.

Try using the 50 Percent Rule. Write your email, count the words, then write it again using half as many. It takes longer to write a shorter email, but your message will have more impact. The shorter your message is, the more likely it is to be read. And bear this in mind: Lincoln's Gettysburg Address contained 272 words. Does your update on the new marketing plan really deserve more than that?

The ideal number of words to use in an email is zero. Meaning: don't send one. Even when someone sends you a message, you don't always need to respond. In the words of David Byrne, "When I have nothing to say, my lips are sealed." You can get away with this more often than you might imagine.

Steve Jobs once said he was as proud of the products he didn't make as he was of the ones he did. I feel that way about the texts and emails I didn't send.

THE STREISAND EFFECT

In 2003, actress and singer Barbra Streisand sued a photographer who had posted aerial photos of her Malibu estate on his website. She claimed the pictures were an invasion of her privacy and demanded that the photographer take them down. But her lawsuit backfired. All of a sudden hundreds of thousands of people who had never stopped to wonder where Barbra Streisand lived decided to visit the site to see the photos. Her efforts drew more attention to the thing she wanted to hide, a phenomenon that has since come to be known as the Streisand Effect.

The lesson: when you are managing conflict, silence is sometimes the best solution, and anything you say or do will squander your power instead of increasing it. The more you talk, the weaker you get. Pulled over by the cops? Say as little as possible. There is zero upside in talking. Even if you have not been given a Miranda warning, anything you say can and probably will be used against you. Getting dragged on the internet? STFU. In 2018, a restaurant in Virginia came under attack after refusing to serve Sarah Huckabee Sanders, press secretary to President Donald Trump. The restaurant's co-owner, a friend of mine, wanted to defend herself, but decided that the best way to manage the crisis was to maintain a stony silence. This wasn't easy—she's a fighter—but her refusal to speak made her powerful. One year after the incident, business was booming.

Savvy lawyers sometimes gain power over their opponents by refusing to respond to messages from the other side. In certain situations, there is nothing you can say that is better than saying nothing. Bret Rappaport, an attorney, urges lawyers to employ "eloquent silence" when communicating with the opposing side; refusing to respond can speak volumes. Rappaport cites linguist William Samarin, one of the first academics to view silence as something more than just empty space. Samarin wrote, "Silence can have meaning. Like the zero in mathematics, it is an absence with a function." Or, as Che Guevara famously said, "Silence is argument carried out by other means."

THE MAGICAL NUMBER SEVEN

Powerful communicators don't just use fewer words; they also break the flow of words into small chunks separated by pauses, which exploits the way our brains work.

More than a half century ago, Harvard psychologist George Miller published one of the most famous papers in the history of the field, titled "The Magical Number Seven, Plus or Minus Two: Some Limits on Our Capacity for Processing Information." Miller determined that our brains hold between five and nine pieces of information in short-term memory at one time and that they break strings of words or numbers into chunks. Stick to Miller's Law—"seven plus or minus two"—and your words will have more impact. Speak in chunks bracketed by pauses. Watch a video of President Barack Obama giving a speech, and you'll see this in action. You don't have to use huge pauses the way Obama does when he's giving a speech to thousands of people. You can be subtler about it. One side benefit of adding those pauses is that it gives you a chance to hold back from saying something you will later great—to be more intentional rather than just machine-gunning away.

THE CEO VERSUS THE CORPORATE RAIDER

Indra Nooyi was one of the greatest big-company CEOs of the past two decades. Whenever someone makes one of those lists of the world's most powerful women, she's always on it, and usually near the top. But chances are you have not heard of her. That's partly because instead of running one of those big Silicon Valley tech companies, Nooyi ran PepsiCo. But it's also because, unlike a lot of those tech bros, Nooyi went out of her way to keep a low profile.

PepsiCo doesn't have the sex appeal of social networks and self-driving cars, but it is an enormous global conglomerate that generates eighty billion dollars in annual sales—more than Tesla and Twitter combined. PepsiCo owns or has owned dozens of other brands, like Taco Bell, Pizza Hut, KFC, Frito-Lay, Tropicana, Quaker Oats, and Gatorade. It's an enormously complex organization, more than a hundred years old, and employs 270,000 people whose livelihoods depend on a CEO to make good decisions.

Taking over a Fortune 500 corporation is a monumental challenge for anyone, but women who climb that mountain face extra challenges. In 2006, when Nooyi took over the reins at PepsiCo, only ten companies in the Fortune 500 had a woman CEO. Out of the entire Fortune 1000, there were only twenty.

Nooyi is not a self-promoter. She didn't shun the press, but she didn't court them, either. (You would be shocked to know how hard many big-company CEOs work to get their picture on magazine covers.) When it came to journalists, "I was always wary," Nooyi recalls in her autobiography. She is congenial, with a disarming smile and a sense of humor. But she is also tough. And smart. She triple-majored in physics, chemistry, and mathematics as an undergraduate, then got a master's degree in business at Yale. It would be a huge mistake to underestimate her, but of course, when she became CEO of PepsiCo, people did.

The most notable was a corporate raider named Nelson Peltz. Peltz is a version of Gordon Gekko but even more of a browbeater. He grew up in Brooklyn, drove trucks for his family's wholesale produce company, and never finished college. Today, he lives in a gaudy, gilded one-hundred-million-dollar Palm Beach estate called Montsorrel with his third wife, a former model. In 2016, he raised a lot of money for his neighbor Donald Trump.

You get the idea.

Peltz made his fortune by bullying his way into companies, splitting them up, and selling off the pieces. He targeted big conglomerates, and he had a "seeming fetish for Fortune 500 companies run by women," Patricia Sellers wrote in *Fortune*, noting that Peltz had gone after Mondelez CEO Irene Rosenfeld and DuPont CEO Ellen Kullman before targeting Nooyi.

Soon after assuming the reins as CEO, Nooyi declared she was taking the company in a new direction. She was going to add healthy food to the product lineup. PepsiCo would become a leader in addressing environmental concerns and sustainability. And, significantly, the company would offer more support for women and families. This wasn't about being nice. It was about being competitive. The plan wasn't going to work right away. Nooyi reckoned it would take ten years to pay off, but if it succeeded, it would set PepsiCo up to thrive for a second century. Instead of obsessing over short-term results, Nooyi was taking a long-term perspective. She was also taking a huge risk. Wall Street doesn't like to be patient. But Nooyi was sure she was doing the right thing.

Sensing her vulnerability, Peltz bought a bunch of PepsiCo stock and launched an attempt at a hostile takeover. He started demanding board seats, hoping to bully Nooyi into selling off divisions so he could grab a quick profit on his stock. He attacked her in the press, criticizing her every decision, seizing on every tiny mistake. He went behind her back and lobbied PepsiCo board members to get rid of her. Nooyi remained unflappable. Whenever Peltz asked for a meeting, she made time for him and listened respectfully. "If you have a great idea, I'd be delighted to listen to it," she told him. "But I have no desire to destroy a great company."

Hoping to get support for his plan on Wall Street, Peltz published a thirty-seven-page open letter explaining his proposal to break up PepsiCo, arguing that investors would make more money if they teamed up against the company.

PepsiCo responded with its own open letter, thanking Mr. Peltz for his interest in the company and assuring him that the board had studied his proposal but had decided to stick with Nooyi's long-term plan.

Peltz kept attacking Nooyi for *three years*. He wanted

to create a sideshow, to put Nooyi into the position of having to defend her strategy and to distract her so that she would spend her time fighting him instead of running the company, and end up making mistakes. But no matter how much Peltz mouthed off, Nooyi never fired back. Why should she? Behind the scenes, she might have been fending off pressure from her board of directors, but in public, when it came to Peltz, she projected a sphinxlike serenity—eloquent silence.

I'm sure this drove him nuts.

Eventually, Nooyi's transformation plan began to work. Sales went up. The stock went up. PepsiCo kept paying a handsome dividend to its investors. Peltz looked like a putz. Instead of reveling in his humiliation, though, Nooyi helped him surrender in a way that let him save face. She and Peltz announced a truce. Nooyi agreed to give a board seat to William Johnson, one of Peltz's advisers. The twist was that Johnson had once been the CEO of Heinz, and during his tenure he had lost a nasty proxy battle with Peltz. Nooyi's message to Peltz could be translated like this: *Sure, we'll give up a board seat, but only to a guy who didn't have the stones to stand up to you.* Nooyi made a public statement thanking Peltz for his "constructive discussions" and "valuable input." Peltz sold his shares and went away.

Nooyi didn't celebrate, or gloat, or brag. She didn't need to. Everybody knew who had won and who had lost. Three years later, in 2018, she retired. In twelve years, she had doubled PepsiCo's market value from $90 billion to $180 billion, which made her one of the best-performing CEOs of her era. *Forbes* named her the world's second-most-powerful woman in the world of business. In 2021, she published her autobiography, in which she devoted only two pages to Peltz. She expressed no rancor or resentment for the way he had treated her. She did, however, point out that, thanks to the success of her plan, Peltz had made a handsome profit on his PepsiCo shares.

That is power.

YOU CAN LEARN A LOT FROM THE MAFIA

In *The Godfather: Part II*, the young Vito Corleone, played by Robert De Niro, asks a neighborhood landlord, Roberto, to change his mind about evicting a woman from her apartment. Roberto tells Corleone to get lost and even threatens to "kick your Sicilian ass into the street." Soon after, Roberto shows up in Corleone's office. People in the neighborhood have told him about Corleone, and now he's terrified. He's babbling. Shaking. He has made a mistake, he says. *Of course*, the woman can stay in her apartment! Corleone says nothing. For ten seconds. Roberto, who previously wanted to raise the woman's rent by five dollars, makes a new offer.

"The rent stays like before," he says.

Corleone still says nothing.

"I'll lower the rent five dollars," Roberto says.

Again, Corleone lets the silence hang.

"Ten dollars, Don Vito."

That's it. The deal is done.

"Ten? *Grazie*," Corleone says.

The two shake hands. Roberto, still babbling, races out the door.

Corleone has the upper hand and is in control of the

situation. He haggles without using words. The longer he waits, the harder the bargain he drives.

Powerful silence runs throughout the Godfather movies. Michael Corleone is as masterful with silence as his father. It's not just in the movies. In real life, Mafia members follow the rule of omertà, a code of silence.

You've probably never heard of Lew Wasserman, but if you worked in Hollywood between 1950 and 1990, you would have lived in fear of him. Charlton Heston called him "the godfather of the movie business," and the connotation was intentional: Wasserman rubbed shoulders with mobsters.

Wasserman ran MCA, an entertainment conglomerate that owned movie studios and record companies and exerted control over radio and TV. Jack Valenti, a movie industry lobbyist, once said, "If Hollywood is Mount Olympus, Lew Wasserman is Zeus." Studio executives were so terrified of Wasserman that some fainted or even threw up when he directed his wrath in their direction.

The real key to Wasserman's success, however, was that he knew how to STFU. Nobody ever knew what he was thinking. He kept people guessing. He rarely gave interviews. He trusted no one and put nothing in writing. He gathered information about everyone around him but gave none back. Wasserman learned this trait from his mentor, a studio boss named Jules Stein, who, as Wasserman's biographer Connie Bruck writes in *When Hollywood Had a King*, was known for "choosing his words as warily as though he had to pay for them."

A conversation is a transaction. It's an exchange of information. Powerful people get more than they spend.

HAIL TO THE UNDERTALKER

The best proof of the connection between power and STFU is Joe Biden. Biden spent more than three decades trying to be elected president of the United States—he first ran in 1988—and every time he ran, he blew himself up by making gaffes. He was the Michelangelo of saying stupid things.

In 2008, he met a reporter of Indian heritage and said, "In Delaware, the largest growth in population is Indian Americans moving from India. You cannot go to a 7-Eleven or a Dunkin' Donuts unless you have a slight Indian accent. Am I right?" At a rally in South Carolina, he called out to a state senator to "Stand up and let the people see you." Then, realizing that the state senator was a paraplegic and confined to a wheelchair: "Oh, God love ya. What am I talking about?"

Biden screwed up so persistently on the 2008 campaign trail that the Republican National Committee started a Joe Biden Gaffe Clock. After Obama chose Biden as his running mate, Biden called him "Barack America." The *New York Times* called Biden a "human verbal wrecking crew," and said, "A day on the campaign trail without a cringe-inducing gaffe is a rare blessing."

Biden was such a Hall of Fame gobshite that when political scientist Stephen Frantzich published a book in 2012 about political gaffes, he put Biden on the cover and said he could not imagine Biden ever developing the discipline needed to become president. Eight years later, in 2020, Biden seemed destined to blow it again. In the first Democratic primary debate, he gaffed, flubbed, and got trounced by the other candidates. But, then, a miracle happened. He changed and became almost a different person. He kept his answers short. He didn't ramble. His handlers kept him away from reporters. When he did talk to the press, he took only a few questions, didn't say much, and made a quick escape.

Biden's transformation "shows the capability of will-power," Frantzich told me. "He had good advisers. He had people teaching him. He realized [that overtalking] was a hurdle he had to overcome. But he wanted the presidency bad enough that he was able to do it." For the advisers who worked with Biden, "It was a combination of teaching him but also of not letting him talk."

Biden continued to wield silence as a weapon after he took office. During the first weeks of 2021 Biden set up calls with foreign leaders, but excluded Israeli prime minister Benjamin Netanyahu—which some interpreted as Biden's way to signal displeasure about Netanyahu's policies and to weaken Netanyahu before an election. The White House denied that Biden was snubbing Netanyahu. Nevertheless, a few months later, in June 2021, Netanyahu was bumped out of office after twelve years of running the country.

SENATOR, YOU'RE NO JACK KENNEDY

The greatest political smackdown in recent memory had only twenty-two words and took only ten seconds to deliver. And that's why it worked.

In a 1988 vice-presidential debate, Senator Lloyd Bentsen, a Democrat, squared off against Senator Dan Quayle, a Republican. Bentsen was sixty-seven years old, a tall Texan who had been serving in Congress since the 1940s.

Quayle was forty-one, an inexperienced lightweight who was not overly burdened with intelligence.

During the debate, the moderator asked Quayle whether he felt he was qualified to serve as president if the job fell to him. Quayle got testy and spent nearly two minutes making a not-very-convincing case for himself—which included the fact that he had as much experience as John F. Kennedy had had when *he* ran for president.

At those words, Bentsen looked like a cat that had just trapped a mouse. When Quayle finished speaking, Bentsen turned, looked directly at him, and said, "Senator, I served with Jack Kennedy. I knew Jack Kennedy. Jack Kennedy was a friend of mine." He paused for two seconds, then delivered the knockout: "Senator, you're no Jack Kennedy."

Boom! The audience burst into applause, a roar that lasted fifteen seconds. Quayle looked like he had had the wind knocked out of him.

In the end, Quayle became vice president, but he never lived down that insult. It was as if Bentsen has slapped him in the face and left a permanent handprint. *Saturday Night Live* started depicting Quayle as a kid sitting on the president's lap. The crack itself has become part of the cultural lexicon. Versions of it have popped up in TV comedies and movies. Megadeth sampled it in a song. It even has its own Wikipedia page.

Bentsen's retort is a master class in how to use fewer words to deliver more power. Bentsen didn't launch into a long-winded description of the differences between Kennedy and Quayle. He didn't argue with facts or spend time going into details to prove that Quayle did not, in fact, have as much experience as Kennedy did when he ran. He merely delivered those twenty-two words. Four short, declarative sentences. He talked less and got more.

THE POWER OF BEING UNDERESTIMATED

For fifteen years, Angela Merkel was the most powerful woman in the world—and possibly the most boring. In private, the German chancellor apparently loved to crack jokes. She even did impersonations of other world leaders. But in public, she pulled down the curtain. She was stoic, dour, unflappable, unemotional, a master of STFU. "Throughout her career, Merkel has made a virtue of biding her time and keeping her mouth shut," George Packer wrote in the *New Yorker*, calling her "the quiet German."

While her egomaniac alpha-male political rivals strutted and preened and gave speeches, Merkel held back and made sure nobody knew what she was thinking. She rose to power by watching, waiting, and studying her opponents while giving away nothing about herself. As one observer said, "It is the absence of charisma that makes her charismatic."

Merkel was the Ambien of politicians, delivering droning speeches that seemed designed to put people to sleep. But her lack of charisma fooled people into underestimating her. Behind her boring facade, she was ruthless. She got her first big break when Chancellor Helmut Kohl took her under his wing and made her part of his cabinet. She got her second big break by choosing an opportune moment to criticize Kohl in the press and replacing him as party chairman nine years later.

A former scientist with a doctorate in physics, Merkel was smarter than the people around her and usually many steps ahead. Yet, in conversations, she let others do almost all the talking. She hated making small talk, did not suffer fools gladly, and banished people who violated her trust. As chancellor, she never used social media, shunned interviews, and even refused to cooperate with a biographer.

"She is a master of listening," an associate once said. "In a conversation, she speaks twenty percent, you speak eighty percent. She gives everybody the feeling *I want to hear what you have to say*, but the truth is that her judgment is made within three minutes, and sometimes she thinks another eighteen minutes are wasted time. She is like a computer—*Is this possible, what this man proposes?* She's able in a very quick time to realize if it's fantasy."

Merkel distrusted Barack Obama's soaring rhetoric and was uncomfortable with him in private because, like her, he kept his thoughts to himself, and she couldn't read him. She knew how to handle tough-talking macho leaders like Russian president Vladimir Putin, but the reserved, cerebral Obama, who did not play the tough guy in public, remained an enigma. He and Merkel were, according to Merkel's associate, "like two hit men in the same room. They don't have to talk—both are quiet, both are killers."

Obama, in fact, knew how to get under Merkel's skin—and like her, he used silence as a weapon. In 2011 and 2012, during a European debt crisis when the US administration felt Merkel was being obstinate and messing things up for the rest of Europe and the rest of the world, Obama stopped talking to her. Merkel's staff would reach out requesting a conversation, and the White House would simply not return the call—a message to Merkel that was loud and clear. In a heated meeting during the crisis,

Obama reportedly upset Merkel so much that she began to cry—proving Obama's own mastery of quiet power.

Merkel understood that saying nothing is the ultimate flex and that when you have power, you don't need to respond to attacks. She would just remain silent and let her opponents punch themselves out. Once, a politician from a tiny left-wing opposition party delivered a blistering speech in the Bundestag, accusing Merkel, to her face, of being a fascist who was operating in "the ruthless old German style." The woman was basically calling Merkel a Nazi—an incendiary charge anywhere, but especially in Germany.

Merkel's allies exploded with anger. A shouting match ensued. Merkel, however, made a point of ignoring the whole thing and looking bored. Her unspoken message: *Rant all you want, I'm still in charge. And thanks very much for ensuring that, in the next election, your powerless party will win even less of the vote. Well done.*

Refusing to respond to attacks works like a shrinking potion. The longer the other person rants, the smaller they become. They're throwing marshmallows at you. Eventually, they start to look ridiculous—like a baby having a tantrum. Even though they may be hurling terrible, hurtful things at you, hoping to provoke a response, ignore the words and focus on the performance. Know that the more they say, the more powerful you become in that relationship. Enjoy the show.

STEVE JOBS, CULT LEADER

I used to write about technology for *Newsweek*. In that racket, you're always trying to get famous CEOs to talk to you, and you quickly become good at measuring someone's power, because you possess a very accurate power barometer: the less someone wants to talk to you, the more powerful they are.

People like Mark Zuckerberg and Jeff Bezos were nearly impossible, and when they did agree to speak to a journalist, they kept things brief and delivered canned, scripted responses. But no one ever wielded as much power over the press as Apple CEO Steve Jobs, and he did it because he was a master of STFU. Jobs was maddening because you knew that if he just opened up and spoke, he would be the most fascinating, brilliant, interesting person you ever met. But he wouldn't do it. And the less he spoke, the more power he accumulated. Because of this, he became the holy grail for business reporters—the once-in-a-lifetime interview.

Apple was built in Jobs's secretive image. The company didn't do publicity; it did anti-publicity. Instead of trying to get coverage, it pushed reporters away. I used to think that working in Apple PR would be the easiest job in the world because you had to say only two words: "No comment."

When Apple introduced a new Mac or iPod, it gave early units to a few carefully selected reviewers, who knew that unless they said good things, they would get bounced off that list in future. Apple rarely got bad reviews. Even when it screwed up—which happened, not often, but sometimes—reporters would bend over backward to make excuses for the company.

This was all Jobs's doing. He was a master at manipulating and controlling people. He was as much a cult leader as he was a CEO. For years, when Apple introduced a new iPhone, customers would start lining up three days in advance. They would sleep on the sidewalk. What other company could inspire such insane devotion?

Once every few years, Jobs would emerge from seclusion and grant an interview. He did this only when he knew exactly what he wanted to say, usually when he was promoting a new product. And he controlled every aspect of the interview.

Most CEOs touting a new product will go on a publicity tour or spend a day sitting in a conference room talking to one reporter after another. Jobs would have none of that, realizing that CEOs who schlepped around to talk to reporters and hired PR people to pitch editors and get them publicity were weak. They were a dime a dozen.

Getting press coverage is like getting a loan from a bank: it's easier to get when you don't need it. "How do I get on *Charlie Rose*?" a tech CEO once asked me. I mumbled something vague, but the unspoken truth was this: *The fact that you're asking this question is the reason you will not get on.*

Jobs knew that his face sold magazines. So he put himself in control by making magazines fight over him. Only one magazine would get the interview. But to be blessed with the privilege to sit in a room with him, there was a price to pay. Apple would play *Time* and *Newsweek* off each other and negotiate with the editors in chief. To score the coveted interview, the magazine had to guarantee that Jobs would be on the cover, obviously. But Apple always pushed for more. What conditions would you agree to? How many pages would you devote to the story? What would you say? Essentially, Apple wanted complete control. It wanted you to turn your magazine into a PR brochure for its products.

These were ridiculous demands. The fact that Apple would even ask for this stuff was shocking, outrageous, unthinkable. Editors do not let story subjects dictate the terms of their coverage, and magazines do not hand over editorial control to the person they are writing about.

But this was Apple. This was Steve Jobs, the Jesus of Silicon Valley. These were his terms. During my time at *Newsweek*, we never got an interview with Jobs. But others did. I have no idea what they gave up to get him.

WHEN WORDS CONFUSE RATHER THAN ENLIGHTEN

When the Supreme Court legalized same-sex marriage in the 2015 *Obergefell v. Hodges* decision, Ruth Bader Ginsburg concurred with the decision but did not completely agree with the reasoning of Justice Anthony Kennedy, who wrote the majority opinion. In such circumstances, justices sometimes write concurring opinions to explain their thoughts on the case. But Ginsburg decided to hold back. She believed that more words would only drain the power of the decision. "It was more powerful to have the same, single opinion," she told an audience at Duke University soon after the decision. "That kind of discipline is to say, 'I'm not the queen, and if the majority is close enough to what I think . . . then I don't have to have it exactly as I would have written it.'"

Ginsburg kept on her shelves a book of unpublished dissents that Justice Louis Brandeis had written but not released. It helped remind her that sometimes it was better to refrain from adding your voice. In *Obergefell*, the four justices opposed to the decision wrote dissenting opinions.

Ginsburg believed those were "bound to spread confusion," and she didn't want to add to that confusion.

Ginsburg knew *Obergefell* would be cited for decades by lawyers and judges who would apply it as a precedent in future cases. She could imagine *Obergefell* from the perspective of future jurists and wanted the decision to be as clear as possible—even if that meant leaving her own voice (and ideas) out of the discussion.

There are two lessons to take away from this. The first is that extra words drain power from a message rather than adding it. The second is that before you speak or write, let your imagination leap to the future and imagine how your words will look then. When you take the long view, you find that a lot of what you want to say can be left out.

POWER MOVES

Most of us are not going to become Supreme Court justices or billionaire CEOs. But we can learn from powerful people and copy their techniques to become more powerful ourselves. Here are some ways to do it:

Pretend words are money. After I read about Lew Wasserman, the godfather of Hollywood, and his mentor Jules Stein, who chose words "as though he had to pay for them," I came up with a game that I call Pretend Words Are Money. Imagine that the conversation you're having is a transaction, and your goal is to get more than you spend. Ask questions and glean information while deflecting questions and giving up as little as possible.

Don't waffle. Perhaps because we want to be polite, or because we feel unsure of ourselves, we constantly give up power by adding "waffle words" that weaken our message. Consider the difference between these two sentences: "I don't think I can pay that much for this car" and "I can't pay that much for this car." Those extra words are called "verbal leaks," meaning you are leaking or revealing something to the other person that tilts the balance of power in their direction. Don't give yourself away. And watch out for verbal leaks when other people speak. You'll give yourself an edge.

Use the Bezos Question Mark Method. Look for every opportunity to respond to or forward an email without adding to it. You won't look arrogant. You'll look busy.

Let people underestimate you. Don't get pulled into the trap of trying to show everyone how smart you are. Be like Angela Merkel—quiet and unassuming. Ultimately, this will play to your advantage.

If you're angry, don't show it. If someone is shouting at you, in person or via email or text, do not shout back. This will infuriate the shouter. "If your enemy is temperamental, seek to irritate him," Sun Tzu said. Stay calm. Bait your enemy into overtalking. Sit there, blank-faced, like Merkel did to the politician who attacked her in the Bundestag. Be happy! They're angry; you're not. You've already won.

Don't fight with people on Twitter. You don't look clever, witty, or domineering. You don't look like an intellectual engaging in a philosophical debate. You look like someone who goes to the zoo to have poo-throwing fights with the monkeys. You cannot win. You're making yourself look foolish and weak. Walk away.

Be vague. Researchers have found that powerful people use more abstract language and don't dwell on details. Diving down into facts and figures doesn't make you look smart; it makes you look weak. Think of Obama's 2008 slogan, "Yes We Can." Or the classic ad tagline from Steve Jobs: "Think different." What did those mean? They meant whatever you wanted them to mean. Vague statements lead people to fill in the blanks with their own hopes and desires. They make people curious and draw them toward you.

Use silence to flatter your superiors. Leaving a brief pause after someone with higher status speaks conveys respect. It's a subtle move but will subconsciously make that person feel secure that you know your place, which also makes them like you a little better. "Always make those above you feel comfortably superior," Robert Greene advises in his book on power. "Make your masters appear more brilliant than they are and you will attain the heights of power." You can also use silence to signal disapproval. When that jerk Larry makes a sexist remark in a meeting, and you don't want to turn it into a confrontation but you also don't want to let it slide—just STFU. All of you. When Larry stops talking, let a long, awkward, uncomfortable pause hang in the air. You're using quiet power to put him in his place, shaming him without saying a word. That's power.

10

STFU AND LISTEN

On a crisp fall afternoon in Boulder, Colorado, with aspen leaves turning yellow and snowcaps glinting off distant mountains against a bright blue sky, fifteen tech start-up founders, strangers to one another, are being paired off and sent into the woods with an assignment: Take turns talking about the one thing you wish your team understood about you. When it's your turn to listen, just listen. No interrupting. No asking questions. No suggesting things the other person might do. Just STFU and listen.

Each of these fifteen aspiring Musks and Zuckerbergs has shelled out ten thousand dollars to spend three days at a boot camp run by Jerry Colonna, an executive coach who has worked with some of the biggest names in Silicon Valley and who gets called things like "the CEO Whisperer" and "the Yoda of Silicon Valley." Once upon a time, Colonna was a successful venture capitalist, but then he went on a two-week vision quest that included wandering naked in a Utah desert without any food, and he came back a different person. He quit Wall Street, moved to Boulder, embraced Buddhism, and reinvented himself as a guru-slash-shaman teaching Silicon Valley big shots how to get in touch with their feelings.

Over the course of this three-day boot camp, Colonna's fifteen-member cohort will spill their guts about fear and shame, and most will end up sobbing. But the main reason they are here is to learn how to STFU and listen. For most of them, this does not come naturally. Most entrepreneurs and CEOs are terrible listeners, way worse than average. They've never listened to anyone. They're type-A Ego Talkers who spend their whole lives in brag mode, telling everyone how smart they are and why their ideas are brilliant. "They might not have full-blown narcissistic personality disorder," says Andy Crissinger, a coach who works for Colonna's firm, Reboot, and who specializes in teaching listening skills, "but they're on the spectrum." Until now, their overweening dickishness has been a kind of superpower. Not many people are cocky enough to walk into a meeting with investors armed with nothing but a PowerPoint deck and a good line of bullshit and walk out with tens or even hundreds of millions of dollars. But once they've raised those millions, things change. Now their job is to build a company, which means hiring people and managing people, and most of them do not possess much in the way of people skills. "All their lives, they've been rewarded for being powerful communicators," says Crissinger. "But now they need to cultivate quieter skills, like asking good questions and listening."

That's where Colonna and his coaches come in. Crissinger has developed a curriculum of listening exercises, and while the magic doesn't happen in three days, the young founders go away armed with some instruction. "Listening isn't easy," Crissinger says. "But it is a very accessible skill set that can be cultivated through practice."

Learning to listen means pushing back against an entire lifetime of being pressured to talk, starting in childhood. In school, you get grades for participation but zero points for being a good listener. "We're not taught how to listen when we're kids, and we're not rewarded for it," says Crissinger. "And we live in this unprecedented time of information proliferation. We're encouraged to be creating content, pushing content, developing a personal brand, pushing things outward, projecting ourselves into the world."

Most of us can't pony up ten grand for a three-day retreat with the Yoda of Silicon Valley, so Colonna offers a free six-day online class about listening skills. You don't get the pretty scenery or the chance to sob in front of a bunch of strangers, but you do get access to some of the exercises he uses with clients.

Colonna is such an intense listener that I found it pretty much impossible to interview him. When we got on Zoom and I asked him a question, instead of answering, he told me to stop taking notes, and then *he* started interviewing *me*. I was determined not to fall for his super-listening guru act, but somehow he got me talking.

When our thirty minutes were up, I realized that I had not asked a single question. Jerry said we could book another time to do the actual interview. I told him, sure, I'd do that, but I knew I would never let myself be exposed to his witchcraft again. Besides, I didn't need to interview him. He had just led me to understand the power of active listening—by showing me instead of telling me.

YOUR BRAIN DOESN'T WANT TO LISTEN

Most people are terrible listeners. Only about 10 percent of the population can listen effectively. On average, we retain only about 25 percent of what we hear, and up to half of what we hear disappears within the first eight hours. The strange thing is that most of us also believe that we are above-average listeners and that it's everybody else who needs help.

It is physiologically difficult to be a good listener. Our brains work too fast—humans speak about 125 words per minute, but our brains can process 800 words per minute—so we focus for a little while, but then our restless brains begin to drift. We start looking at our phones and laptops, or dreaming up plans for the weekend, or thinking about what we're going to say as soon as this other person finally stops saying whatever it is they're saying, which right now seems to be *mwah mwah mwah*, like the adults in a Charlie Brown cartoon.

I've put listening at the end of the book because of all the disciplines I've adopted as part of STFU, learning how to become an active listener is by far the most challenging. The other exercises—saying nothing when possible, enduring awkward silences, spending time in silence, avoiding social media—lay the foundation for listening. You can't be a great active listener without first conquering the other challenges.

Active listening is exhausting. It requires a huge amount of focus, and it's not easy to rein in our brains, which have evolved with an urge to wander. That urge has served us well. If our brains didn't wander, we would have no civilization, no science, no Beethoven symphonies, no *Real Housewives.*

When you're listening actively, you are forcing your brain to do something it was not designed to do. Curbing that urge is especially difficult for compulsive overtalkers, because our brains are more restless than most, and even with the help of meds, someone who suffers from ADHD is going to struggle. People like me find it nearly impossible to talk to someone on the phone without doing something else—texting, reading emails, skimming headlines on the *New York Times* website—at the same time. We get jittery and anxious. We feel physically upset. We want desperately to make this bad feeling go away, and so, we open our laptop or grab the remote.

I've spent the past year working on my listening skills, and I am much better than I used to be, but I still find myself drifting. I find it nearly impossible to stay focused during Zoom meetings, especially if there are several people on the call. In my defense, it seems that nobody else can pay attention on Zoom, either. There's even a name for it: Zoom fatigue. Supposedly this happens because our brains are working overtime to fill in information that we usually pick up unconsciously from body language and facial expression cues.

Another challenge is that active listening never gets easy. It's not like riding a bike, where once you learn how to do it, it becomes automatic. Active listening is more like lifting weights. Over time you get stronger, but it always requires effort. Business guru Tom Peters, coauthor of *In Search of Excellence*, says if you're not completely wiped out after thirty minutes of active listening, you're not doing it right. Peters also says that almost every great business leader he has ever met—and he has met almost all of them, and studied them, and advised some of them—possesses an Olympic-level ability to engage in what he calls "aggressive listening."

THE SMARTEST-KID-IN-CLASS SYNDROME

Learning how to listen might not get you a job running a Fortune 500 company, but it will help you do your job better and improve your chances of being promoted. It will make you smarter and more likable. It will also, paradoxically, make it more likely that people will consider you a sparkling conversationalist.

Not listening, however, can lead to some disastrous outcomes. Some of the worst listeners in the world are the people who should be the best: doctors. On average, doctors wait only eighteen seconds before they interrupt a patient. This astonishing figure was first reported by Dr. Jerome Groopman in 2007, in a book called *How Doctors Think*.

If you know any doctors, you will understand why they are such terrible listeners. I happen to have a few friends and family members who are doctors, and I love them to death, but a lot of doctors suffer from Smartest-Kid-in-Class Syndrome. They have gone through life always being the kid at the top of the class, the one who gets nothing but praise from teachers and parents. Then they go to med school, with a bunch of other smartest kids in class, and they spend their lives doing a job where they always know more than the people who come to them for help. This makes them predisposed to think that they are smarter than everyone around them *in any situation*. All this is compounded by the fact that, for some reason, a lot of people who are drawn to medicine tend to have high IQs but low EQs, or "emotional quotients." They know how to fix people but have no idea how to *listen* to them. So, you walk in, start to explain what's going on, and the Smartest Kid in Class cuts you off, because he already knows what's wrong and how to fix it. The problem is that about 20 percent of the time, doctors make the wrong diagnosis. Go in with a heart attack, and they'll tell you it's acid reflux and send you home with an antacid. Whoops!

Groopman's "18-Second Rule" was widely cited and should have been a wake-up call to the medical profession, but fifteen years later, thanks to managed care, not much has changed. In fact, doctors are under even greater pressure to crank through as many patients as they can in as little time as possible. Those eighteen seconds might now be twelve.

The fear that patients will talk too much and slow things down is mostly unfounded. Researchers have found that when doctors do not interrupt, patients don't prattle on for long—only about ninety seconds on average. That's a small price to pay to avoid making a wrong diagnosis. Other studies have found that empathic listening can even help patients recover from aches and pains. Patients who are given a placebo but who spend a few minutes talking to a nurse or doctor claim that their backache or leg pain has decreased.

At least superficially, the medical profession has acknowledged the importance of listening. Programs have sprung up to teach doctors and nurses how to listen. But not much has changed. "There has been a lot of activity, so they think they are doing better," says Helen Meldrum, a researcher who specializes in listening skills in the medical profession. "But the clinical medical and nursing schools do not teach the skills in a manner that actually affects behavior." A lot of doctors think communication skills are bullshit or a waste of time, and their training reinforces that idea. Many doctors come out of med school with less empathy than when they went in.

Next time you see a doctor, set a timer on your phone. If the doc lets you speak your piece, great. If you get cut off after eighteen seconds, or even less time than that, you might want to get a second opinion.

THE DEVIL WEARS PRADA—AND DOESN'T LISTEN

Being a bad listener can cost you plenty, as Anna Wintour, the dictatorial editor in chief of *Vogue*, learned in 2020. Wintour's ability to remain silent enabled her to accumulate power, but that power, and a seeming inability to take advice from people around her, almost ended her career.

Wintour is by most accounts a terrifying person. Her nickname is "Nuclear Wintour," and she was the model for the mean-boss title character in *The Devil Wears Prada*. She wears enormous sunglasses, even indoors, even during interviews, like a cartoon movie villain, "to hide what she's really thinking or feeling," according to her biographer. The shades also declare to the world that she has no interest in what anyone else has to say—the worst message any leader can send.

Wintour has run *Vogue* for more than three decades, and she's also the editorial director for all Condé Nast publications, which makes her one of the most powerful people in both the media business and the fashion industry. Her employees fear her so much that they do not dare speak to her or even look at her unless she speaks to them.

In a bygone era, companies tolerated leaders who didn't listen. But in a new era, employees are more empowered, including those at *Vogue*. As Wintour's biographer Amy Odell writes, "Anna's way or the highway . . . wasn't something they were going to accept."

In 2020, after the police killings of Breonna Taylor and George Floyd, rank-and-file staffers at *Vogue* went public with complaints that Wintour had not done enough to elevate Black voices, had not hired enough Black employees, and had published hurtful images. Wintour had publicly supported the Black Lives Matter movement and had a diversity and inclusion council, but some employees believed she had not backed that up with action inside Condé Nast or in the pages of *Vogue*. Her "management style didn't align with these progressive stances," Odell writes.

For years, Wintour had been warned that dissent was brewing, that the world was changing, and that *Vogue* needed to change with it. But she ignored these warnings and kept making mistakes. Urged to work with diverse models, Wintour "made comments like 'Don't we have enough gays?'—or 'enough men' or 'enough lesbians' or 'enough Black people'—in this issue?" Odell writes. In 2017, against the advice of her editors, Wintour went ahead with a shoot in which supermodel Karlie Kloss was dressed as a geisha, and then seemed baffled when the photos created an uproar. Soon after, *Vogue* shot model Gigi Hadid wearing leisure clothes with a group of Black basketball players installed as background props, a decision that was "surprisingly tone-deaf by 2017," Odell writes. "It wasn't clear that Anna fully grasped what was problematic when it came to race." Her "management style had never seemed more mismatched for a particular moment," and her dictatorial style "seemed now like a liability, perhaps as it should have been all along." Suddenly, people were saying the unthinkable, that Anna Wintour—*the invincible Anna Wintour!*—should resign. "Can Anna Wintour Survive the Social Justice Movement?" the *New York Times* wondered.

Condé Nast did not force Wintour to step down. I'm not sure anyone inside the company would dare try. They're all terrified of her. Then again, others have been taken down for less. Wintour saved herself by apologizing to staff in an email in which she admitted she had made mistakes and accepted responsibility for them. Her public act of contrition invoked the magic word *listen*. "I am listening," she wrote, "and would like to hear your feedback and your advice."

Right. Sure. Dame Anna Wintour would love to hear your feedback. She promises not to call you fat or stupid or make fun of your clothes. She swears you won't get fired. Who wants to go first?

Soon after sending the email, Wintour went on a podcast to hammer the listening message home: "What one needs to do as a leader is really just hear. Listen and hear and act. I wasn't listening. Or listening enough. I think what's important is to be seen as someone who does listen and that will hear any number of complaints or questions or suggestions."

In case you missed it: she's *listening*. Or at least *hopes to be seen* as someone who is listening.

It must have pained her to adopt the persona of the

humble leader. The idea that "Nuclear Wintour" would learn how to listen, even a little bit, seems about as likely as her moving to Calcutta to care for orphans and lepers. But she knew what she had to say, and she said it. Maybe that's progress?

TIM COOK, THE QUIET CEO

Tim Cook, the CEO of Apple, has been called the world's greatest leader. He's also one of the world's greatest listeners, a superpower he uses to his advantage.

On the surface, Cook is a reserved, soft-spoken guy, an Alabama native with a trace of a southern accent, and he generally doesn't say much. He is the polar opposite of his predecessor, Steve Jobs, the cofounder of Apple, who loved to antagonize people: "That idea is shit. It's the dumbest thing I've ever heard" was a typical Jobs remark. Jobs believed he would elicit the best information by prompting an argument or a debate. He wanted to make you defend your idea by turning a meeting into a shouting match, an intellectual battle. If you couldn't stand up to him, you were toast.

Cook seems to believe he'll get more and better information if he sits back and lets people talk. He doesn't do this to be polite, but because it sometimes leads them to reveal things they might not want to tell him. Like Jobs, Cook is trying to get to the truth. He's just taking a different route.

Cook is such a master that even when people prepare to defend themselves against his dark arts, he can still get them talking using nothing but body language, facial expressions, nods, and a few well-placed *hmmm*s and *aha*s.

My friend Kim Malone Scott, an executive coach in Silicon Valley, learned this when she interviewed for a job at Apple and had to meet with Cook. "A friend of mine warned me before I went there to talk to Tim," Scott said. "He told me, 'Look, Tim is very quiet. He will drag you out onto a conversational limb where you don't want to go. So, be careful.'"

Scott is gregarious and kind of an overtalker, but she resolved to keep herself under control. Before the meeting, as she sat outside Cook's office, she gave herself one last reminder to proceed with caution. *Think before you speak. Don't start rambling. Stay focused.* She didn't have any deep secret she needed to hide, but she wanted to make a good impression.

The two sat down on comfortable chairs across from each other, made some small talk, and then Cook asked her one question: "I think it's great when people decide to make a career change. Why are you doing it?" That was all he said. Then he sat back and listened. He wasn't overly friendly, but he wasn't unfriendly. He was inscrutable.

Scott knew he was paying attention, but she couldn't tell what he was thinking. So, she talked. And kept talking. After a few minutes, she realized that she was still talking—and worse, for reasons unknown, she was telling Cook about some huge mistake she made when she was working at Google. "I kind of snapped out of it and pulled up and said to myself, *Wait, why am I telling him this? How did I get here? If I don't shut up right now, I'm going to talk myself out of this job.*"

Scott still doesn't know how Cook worked his magic on her. She had walked into the meeting determined to STFU and be careful, to speak with intention, and yet, there she was, way out on a limb, just where her friend had warned her she might wind up.

The good news is that Cook liked her, and she got the job. The even better news is that Scott learned a lesson about the power of listening, one she applies when she manages people. If you sit and back and let them talk, eventually they will tell you the truth. "That's when you learn the things that people don't want to tell you. Or, sometimes, the things you don't want to know."

Since then, Scott has written two books about interpersonal relationships at work. She developed a management concept she calls "radical candor"—it's also the title of one of her books—and believes in being almost brutally direct and honest with people at work.

Scott offers another piece of STFU-related advice: "Leave three unimportant things unsaid every day." This applies in the workplace but also in romantic partnerships. "Leaving things unsaid is all about not nitpicking," she says. "Our minds are filters, and we are happier when we let our minds ignore unimportant things."

LEADERS WHO LISTEN

J. W. "Bill" Marriott Jr., the billionaire head of the Marriott hotel company, probably knows more about hospitality than almost anyone in the world. He has spent his whole life in the business, having learned from his father, who started the company. Despite his expertise, Marriott spends most of his time asking questions and listening to other people. His famous mantra? "The four most important words in the English language are 'What do you think?'"

Barack Obama says the first thing he learned as a community organizer is that "you show up in a neighborhood and your initial instinct is to tell people what they should be interested in, instead of spending the first six months *listening* and find[ing] out what they actually *are* interested in."

Richard Branson, the founder of Virgin Group, made his billions by hiring smart people and then listening to them as well as to his customers. From his earliest days running a record shop in London, and then as the head of a record label, Branson possessed a keen ability to listen to people and figure out what they wanted. That skill led him to expand his empire into airlines, railways, space travel, and other businesses.

Branson's public persona as a free-spirited daredevil, an inveterate showboater and self-promoter with long blond hair and movie star looks, is a bit misleading. In private, Branson is a fierce listener who lets everyone else do all the talking. He says he became a good listener out of necessity: he has dyslexia, and he got through school by listening rather than reading.

In fact, a lot of successful entrepreneurs are dyslexic. I suspect that, like Branson, they developed powerful listening skills when they were kids and that this ability served them well as they entered the business world. When Branson sat down to write a book about how to manage people—*The Virgin Way: Everything I Know About Leadership*—he devoted a third of it to the art of listening. One money quote: "Nobody ever learned anything from listening to themselves speak."

Another of Branson's listening tricks: take notes. He

carries a notebook with him at all times and encourages his employees to do the same. Taking notes forces you to focus on what's being said and demonstrates to the person speaking that you are paying attention and that you care about what they say.

LAWYERS WHO LISTEN

When Steven A. Cash worked as an assistant district attorney in New York City, "we had two adages," he told me. "'Tires leave tracks' and 'Nobody ever says nothing.'" The first adage means, literally, that if you use a car in the commission of a crime, you're going to get caught. The second means that a prosecutor can get a confession by sitting back and listening, because suspects "always want to talk," Cash says. "I never had anyone not talk to me. Nobody, when I Mirandized them, ever said, 'I want my lawyer, I don't want to talk to you.' A lot of my interrogations were just me saying, literally, 'So, tell me what happened.' Then I have the tape recorder going, and I just sit back and go, 'Uh-huh, okay,' and I'm just listening to them. Nobody ever said nothing." In the movies, lawyers are great orators, people who can get up and give stirring closing arguments. But in day-to-day lawyering, the game is about listening.

Cash once broke a kidnapping case by letting the suspect talk about mundane things—when he had breakfast, what he had for breakfast, what kind of bagel he ate. The suspect denied committing the crime, but when he talked, he revealed a bizarre verbal tic: He had a habit of saying "boom" at the end of his sentences. *So, I go the store and get the paper, boom. I go home and eat a bagel, boom.* When prosecutors listened to recordings of the ransom calls, the kidnapper had the same verbal tic, saying "boom" at the end of every sentence. Other than the verbal tic, "we didn't have a lot on him," Cash recalls. "But I believe he went away for a long time." The same listening skills were vital, Cash told me, when he later became an intelligence officer at the CIA. He wouldn't go into details, but it's easy to understand how listening and getting people to talk might be sort of central to that line of work.

Today, Cash is a corporate attorney who spends a lot of time preparing and coaching people who are going to testify in front of a jury or judge, speak to the FBI, or be deposed in civil lawsuits. The key thing he teaches is to listen to the question you're asked and to answer *only* that question. "You have to focus very carefully," he says. "People often are not really listening to the question that is being asked. They've stopped listening to the question, and they're ready to answer what they think the question was going to be."

This doesn't mean lying. It means finding a way to answer the question truthfully without offering anything extra. Most people find this incredibly difficult to do, because it's not how we speak in our day-to-day lives. Cash offers an example: Someone asks, "Do you know what time it is?" The polite answer, the one you would use in ordinary conversation, is "Yes, it's three o'clock." The answer you should use as a witness is "Yes."

THE PROFESSOR OF LISTENING

Armed with inspiration, I searched for someone who could show me how to STFU and listen, and I found Sandra Bodin-Lerner, who teaches a course in listening at Kean University in New Jersey. She admits it's an unusual subject.

"I'll tell people that I teach listening, and they always go, 'What? What?' I get that joke a lot," she said. The other common response: wives want their husbands to enroll, and husbands say the same about their wives. "It's easy to recognize it in everybody else, right?" Bodin-Lerner told me. "We think everybody else sucks at listening. Most of us don't realize that it's us, too."

We spoke over Zoom, which I knew would make it difficult for me to remain focused. Before the call, I did my little preparation ritual: deep breaths, reminders to maintain eye contact and pay attention. And I recorded the call, so I wouldn't be distracted by taking notes.

And yet: I blew it.

The problem was not that I lost focus. It was that I could not STFU. When I looked at the transcript of the recording, I found that in our one-hour conversation, I had done about 80 percent of the talking. There, in front of me, on the page, were huge blocks of me babbling away. It's never fun to read a transcript of yourself speaking, but this was especially brutal. I emailed Bodin-Lerner and told her that (a) I was mortified; (b) I was in awe of her listening wizardry and the rope-a-dope she had pulled on me; and (c) I needed to interview her again.

The next time we talked, I succeeded. I had been practicing a lot since our first conversation and took some pride in the fact that I seemed to be making progress. But I also noticed something odd, which was that even on this call, where I thought I had done very little talking, the transcript revealed several places where I spoke a bunch of sentences, usually the type that begin "Yeah, the same thing happened to me . . ."

This is one of the big distractions Bodin-Lerner teaches students to look out for, the urge to tell your own story to match one you've just heard. Others include the urge to give advice and the urge to prove you're smart. There's also the one where, instead of listening, you're thinking about what you're going to say next, and the one where you have this great idea, and if you don't share it right away, you'll forget it.

Bodin-Lerner makes her living primarily as a public speaking coach, but for the past twenty years she has had a side gig lecturing at Kean about interpersonal communication, which basically amounts to teaching people how to do better in relationships, whether that's business, social, or romantic. But she realized that listening was a large—and largely overlooked—part of that. "There would always be one chapter in the textbook about listening, and that was it."

Her department gave her the green light to create a course devoted solely to listening. Seven years later, the course is always oversubscribed, and her students love her. Out of thirty-five ratings on Rate My Professors, twenty-seven scored her as "awesome." One student wrote, "This is the most beneficial course I have taken all throughout college." Bodin-Lerner says her listening course remains one of the only of its kind in the country.

"The main thing I'm teaching is that listening has to be intentional," she said. "You have to choose to do it. You have to tell yourself, 'I'm going to hold back from my need to speak. When something triggers an idea or emotion in me, I'm going to control my need to express it right now.' The first step is just becoming aware, being conscious about listening. And look, listening is super hard. It takes so much mental effort. It's exhausting."

One technique she makes students practice: Before a conversation, resolve to be the "first listener" and let the other person speak before you do. Something amazing happens when you listen and pay fierce attention. The other person becomes more interesting. It's not that they *seem* more interesting, but they actually *are* more interesting. "There's research on this. People open up and communicate better when they're actually listened to. It makes sense if you think about it," Bodin-Lerner says.

One of Bodin-Lerner's recent students was a chatterbox who complained that her boyfriend was uncommunicative. Bodin-Lerner sent her home with an assignment to spend time with her boyfriend while forcing herself to only listen. "She came back to class with a revelation: 'Oh my God, it turns out that if I shut up and listen, he actually has a lot of interesting stuff to say!'"

As a final assignment for the semester, Bodin-Lerner instructs her students to sit through a conversation with someone they find difficult to talk to or someone who holds opinions that are wildly different from their own and listen until they learn something new and interesting about that person. It's excruciating, "but they always come back with some huge piece of information that they had no idea about because they only perceived that person as irritating and annoying." The record holder for biggest revelation was a student who discovered her dad had fought in the Nicaraguan Revolution, been captured, and escaped. Somehow, he had never mentioned this—maybe because nobody was ever listening.

Students always ask if they can bring their friends and family members to class, so Bodin-Lerner sets aside a day for this. "They're always like, 'Oh, can I bring my mom? Because she's a terrible listener.' They see how listening can impact their lives, and then they promote it. They're like, 'Wow, everybody needs to take a listening course.' It's awesome."

One student brought her parents, who were going through a divorce. The visit didn't save their marriage, but maybe it helped them understand each other a little better. Students share a lot of personal information with one another. It's not quite group therapy, but almost. "It's actually beautiful," Bodin-Lerner says. "By the end of the term they feel very close to one another."

Bodin-Lerner helps run the Minnesota-based International Listening Association, which is a real thing and boasts hundreds of members from around the world. The ILA offers training courses that bestow the title of "certified listening professional," publishes a newsletter called the *Listening Post*, sponsors an International Day of Listening, and even has a Listening Hall of Fame and an annual convention. "People say, 'Hey, those conventions must be pretty quiet,'" Bodin-Lerner says. "Everybody says that."

When I first tried to imagine an ILA convention, I pictured a Wes Anderson movie, with goateed men wearing turtlenecks (Hall of Famers) milling about in a hotel ballroom, out-listening one another. But Bodin-Lerner let me sit in on an ILA monthly workshop, and the members were surprisingly (and, I admit, disappointingly) normal and not weird. A doctor in England talked about listening skills in the medical field.

Listening has become a thing in the corporate world, and companies have started hiring Bodin-Lerner to run workshops for employees. She says companies need to realize the role that listening plays in making progress on other issues. "We're constantly told that we need to have these difficult conversations about diversity, equity, and inclusion, that we need to listen to each other. But nobody is teaching us how to do that," she said.

CLIMBING THE LISTENING LADDER

Aspiring leaders take Dale Carnegie courses hoping to learn how to become great public speakers . . . only to discover that Carnegie considered listening to be as important as speaking: "Listen first. Give your opponent a chance to talk. Let them finish. Do not resist, defend, or debate. This only raises barriers."

In *How to Win Friends & Influence People*, Carnegie defines a "listening ladder," which comprises five levels of listening:

1. *Ignoring.* You are not interested at all.
2. *Pretending.* You're nodding, smiling, but you're paying zero attention.
3. *Selecting.* In computer terms, you devote only part of your microprocessing power to the conversation. Instead of processing the full content stream, you're hunting for key words and using them to extrapolate what the person is saying.
4. *Attending.* This is what others call active listening.

5. *Empathizing.* This is Zen master stuff, where you're listening so closely that you feel like you're inside the other person's head.

When you're having a conversation, become conscious of where you are on the ladder and try to work your way up the rungs. Then hang on to that final rung for as long you can. Most people can get to level four and stay there for a while. Getting to level five? Well, I'm working on it.

LISTENING LESSONS

Listening sets a virtuous cycle in motion. The more you listen, the less you talk. The less you talk, the more time you can devote to listening. It's one of those skills that you never fully master. Over time, it becomes more natural, but it always requires effort and concentration.

One way to begin is by doing listening exercises. Sit with a partner and have them tell you a story. Take no notes while they're speaking. Just listen. Once they're done, write down everything you remember, or try to tell the story back to them, and see how your version compares to what the person actually said. This seems easy, but you will probably remember less than you would expect. Doing this exercise again and again will build your listening skills.

You can also try the Three-Question Game, which Andy Crissinger at Reboot uses with clients. Find a partner and begin with each of you writing down three open-ended questions to ask the other. For three minutes, one person asks and the other answers. Then you switch roles. The listener must remain silent through the entire three minutes.

If the speaker finishes talking before the three minutes are up, you sit in silence for the remainder of the time.

Once you have both taken your turn, spend four minutes talking about how it felt to sit and just listen. What was it like to be the listener? What was it like to be the speaker? What did you learn from what they told you? What did you notice? What came up for you?

Here are a few other techniques that can make you a better listener:

Put away your phone. When Christine Lagarde became president of the European Central Bank, she issued an order to the twenty-four commissioners on the governing council: no more phones or iPads allowed in meetings. Unlike her predecessor, Mario Draghi, who spent a lot of time looking at his phone and iPad when others were talking, Lagarde talks very little and listens a lot. She demands the same from others.

Schedule breaks between Zoom calls. If possible, do not schedule back-to-back meetings. But if you cannot do that, take a five-minute break. Get up from your desk and walk around without looking at a screen. This will give you a little bit of energy to help focus during the next call.

Prepare yourself. Before you walk into a coffee shop to meet a friend, take a minute to center yourself. Sit in the car and take a few deep breaths. Relax. Calm down. Jerry Colonna at Reboot calls this "self-soothing." Before you can listen to the other person, you need to get yourself into the right frame of mind: open, receptive, ready for whatever happens.

Imagine you are an improv actor. Improv actors famously use a technique called "Yes, and," which means that no matter what someone says, you begin by agreeing and then go on from there. (Beginning with no has a way of shutting down the skit.) Improv is all about listening and bouncing off what the other person says. Don't go into a conversation with planned comments. Don't force an agenda. Let the conversation go wherever it wants to go.

Ask questions. This is how you get someone talking. Question asking is an art form unto itself, and it might take some practice to learn how to do it. Make your questions open-ended. Resist the urge to interrupt. Don't think about what you're going to say when the other person finishes speaking.

Use body language. Show the other person that you're listening. Lean toward them. Nod. Smile. Don't scowl. Don't make expressions that show disagreement or disapproval. More than half of communication involves body language. Keep an open stance, with your arms uncrossed. Sit still. Fidgeting conveys to the speaker that you're distracted. The effort required to *show* that you're listening will force you to listen.

Give yourself reminders. I keep a note posted above my computer—"LISTEN!"—so I see it whenever I'm on a videoconference or phone call. Tom Peters writes the same thing on the back of his hand.

Record yourself. Have a conversation and record what you say, then send it out to be transcribed. (There are online sites where you can get this done cheaply.) Read the transcript and see how you did. The first thing you'll notice is how sloppy conversations are. But you will also have a visual representation of how much of the conversation you took up. This has been a painful but also eye-opening exercise for me, one that ultimately helped me STFU and listen.

AND NOW YOU'RE PERFECT

Benjamin Franklin once set out to attain moral perfection by creating a list of thirteen virtues and practicing each one in turn. The second virtue on his list was silence, which came with this admonition: "Speak not but what may benefit others or yourself; avoid trifling conversation."

Franklin put silence high on his list of self-improvements because, he confessed, he was an overtalker with a habit of "prattling, punning, and joking, which only made me acceptable to trifling company." He believed that developing the discipline to STFU would make him a better person and enable him to gain knowledge, which was "obtain'd rather by the use of the ears than of the tongue."

It's unclear how well Franklin succeeded at remaining silent, but he did go on to accomplish great things. He also seems to have developed a dislike of overtalkers—which is also what has happened to me. When I began this journey, I loved meeting fellow overtalkers, with whom I could indulge my addiction. Now they annoy the hell out of me.

I'm like the smoker who quits and then can't stand to be around smokers.

As I was finishing this book, I took the Talkaholic Scale test again to see if I had made progress. This time, instead of getting fifty points, the highest possible score, I ended up with forty, which is only borderline talkaholic. Better yet, my wife's assessment of me worked out to thirty-eight. To be sure, the test is not that scientific, and the results might be influenced by bias and wishful thinking. But I do believe I've made progress.

I still find myself blabbing sometimes, and I still catch myself launching into Danalogues—but at least I catch myself. Talking less might never come naturally to me. Probably it will always require effort and concentration. But I slip up far less often than in the past, and I feel the benefits every day.

Having gained more self-control, I find myself to be less anxious, less angry, less prone to outbursts, and better able to "be a little deaf," as Ruth Bader Ginsburg said. I've rolled back the Anxiety Wheel. I've become a better listener and a better parent, far less likely to annoy my kids by delivering a Danalogue or to embarrass them by overtalking to strangers. Interestingly, my wife, Sasha, has changed, too. These days when she and I are out together in social situations, I'm the quiet one, and she talks way more than she used to. It's as if my learning how to STFU has given her a chance to shine. Though I began this journey hoping to fix myself, I discovered that the real power of STFU is that, with it, I could help the people around me and make their lives better, too.

I have found opportunities to spend time in silence and

have developed the discipline to sit with someone and feel connected without saying a word—what the Japanese call "belly talk." I spend less time on small talk and intentionally devote more effort to having meaningful, substantive conversations, the kind that psychologist Matthias Mehl calls "a key ingredient to a satisfied life."

My world contains less noise and more joy, fewer regrets and more peace. Basically, I'm happier. I hope that when you put down this book, you will non-talk your way into happiness, too.

ACKNOWLEDGMENTS

In the spirit of STFU, I will try to keep this brief. But I am forever indebted to the many people who took time to speak with me during the reporting of this book, without whom it would not have been possible. These include Virginia Richmond, who became a friend; Michael Beatty at the University of Miami, a fellow talkaholic who is as entertaining as he is informative; and Matthias Mehl, who taught me how to have "meaningful and substantive conversations" by having a bunch of them with me. Thanks also to Katie Donovan, Sandra Bodin-Lerner, Amos Clifford, Jason Axsom, Jerry Colonna, Andy Crissinger, Kim Malone Scott, Todd Lynch, and others who offered advice, information, and guidance.

Thanks to my agent, Christy Fletcher, and my editor, James Melia, who knew what the book was about even when I did not. A big thanks to Amy Einhorn and everyone else at Henry Holt and Company: Caitlin O'Shaughnessy, Laura Flavin, Pat Eisemann, Omar Chapa, Christopher Sergio, Morgan Mitchell, Kenn Russell, Janel Brown, and

Jason Reigal. Additional thanks to Jenna Dolan and Mark Lerner. Also, I would like to offer special thanks to Lori Kusatzky for her patience, wisdom, and effort.

Most of all, thanks to my family. I'm blessed to have you.

NOTES

INTRODUCTION

5 **avoided it as much as possible:** Paul Halpern, "Einstein Shunned Phones in Favor of Solitude and Quiet Reflection," Medium, August 29, 2016, https://phalpern.medium.com/einstein-shunned-phones -in-favor-of-solitude-and-quiet-reflection-d708deaa216b.

8 **help us grow brain cells:** Imke Kirste et al., "Is Silence Golden? Effects of Auditory Stimuli and Their Absence on Adult Hippo-campal Neurogenesis," *Brain Structure and Function* 220, no. 2 (2013): 1221–28, https://doi.org/10.1007/s00429-013-0679-3.

THE TALKAHOLIC SCALE

11 **the following self-scored questionnaire:** James C. McCroskey and Virginia Richmond, "Identifying Compulsive Communica-tors: The Talkaholic Scale," *Communication Research Reports* 10, no. 2 (1993): 107–14.

1: WHAT WE TALK ABOUT WHEN WE TALK ABOUT OVERTALKING

22 **different kinds of overtalking:** Crystal Raypole, "Has Anyone Ever Said You Talk Too Much? It Might Just Be Your

Personality," Healthline, February 16, 2021, https://www
.healthline.com/health/talking-too-much#is-it-really-too-much.

24 **milder form of the disorder**: Diana Wells, "Pressured Speech
Related to Bipolar Disorder," Healthline, December 6, 2019,
https://www.healthline.com/health/bipolar-disorder/pressured
-speech.

25 **region of the prefrontal cortex**: Michael J. Beatty et al., "Communication Apprehension and Resting Alpha Range Asymmetry in
the Anterior Cortex," *Communication Education* 60, no. 4 (2011):
441–60, https://doi.org/10.1080/03634523.2011.563389.

28 **American Psychiatric Association**: "Americans' Overall Level
of Anxiety About Health, Safety and Finances Remain High,"
American Psychiatric Association, May 20, 2019, https://www
.psychiatry.org/newsroom/news-releases/americans-overall-level
-of-anxiety-about-health-safety-and-finances-remain-high.

28 **full-blown anxiety disorder**: Facts & Statistics, Anxiety and
Depression Association of America, ADAA, n.d., https://adaa.org
/understanding-anxiety/facts-statistic.

2: SITFO: SHUT IT THE FUCK OFF

32 **checked their phone while having sex**: "The Attachment
Problem: Cellphone Use in America," SureCall, n.d., https://www
.surecall.com/docs/20180515-SureCall-Attachment-Survey
-Results-v2.pdf.

32 *eighty-seven* **movies in 2022**: Kasey Moore, "Netflix Unveils
Slate of 87 New Movies Coming in 2022," What's on Netflix, February 10, 2022, https://www.whats-on-netflix.com/news/netflix
-unveils-slate-of-87-new-movies-coming-in-2022/.

32 **plus forty shows**: Reed Gaudens, "Full List of Netflix Shows
Confirmed for Release in 2022," Netflix Life, FanSided, January
27, 2022, https://netflixlife.com/2022/01/27/full-list-netflix-shows
-confirmed-release-2022/.

32 **$17 billion to produce**: "Top US Media Groups Including Disney, Netflix Look to Spend $115B in 2022: FT," Yahoo!, n.d., https://www .yahoo.com/video/top-us-media-groups-including-105112204.html #:~:text=Netflix%20Inc%20(NASDAQ%3A%20NFLX),cash%20 flow%20positive%20in%202022.

32 **according to Nielsen**: G. Winslow, "Streaming Is Up, but Consumers Are Overwhelmed by 817K Available Titles," TVTechnology, April 6, 2022, https://www.tvtechnology.com/news/streaming -up-but-consumers-are-overwhelmed-by-817k-available-titles.

32 **that's 437 hours**: Chris Melore, "Average Consumer Cutting 3 Streaming Services from Their Lineup in 2022," Study Finds, May 6, 2022, https://www.studyfinds.org/cutting-subscriptions -streaming-tv/.

32 **streaming services as we did in 2015**: Julia Stoll, "U.S. Household Expenditure on Streaming and Downloading Video 2020," Statista, January 17, 2022, https://www.statista.com/statistics /1060036/us-consumer-spending-streaming-downloading-video/.

33 **over 100 decibels**: Cara Buckley, "Working or Playing Indoors, New Yorkers Face an Unabated Roar," *New York Times*, July 20, 2012, https://www.nytimes.com/2012/07/20/nyregion/in-new-york -city-indoor-noise-goes-unabated.html.

33 **loud as a jackhammer**: "Noise Sources and Their Effects," https://www.chem.purdue.edu/chemsafety/Training/PPETrain /dblevels.htm.

33 *Barney* **theme song**: Justin Caba, "Torture Methods with Sound: How Pure Noise Can Be Used to Break You Psychologically," Medical Daily, January 21, 2015, https://www.medicaldaily .com/torture-methods-sound-how-pure-noise-can-be-used-break -you-psychologically-318638#:~:text=Sound%20torture%20 is%20a%20type,torture%20under%20the%20right%20conditions.

33 **force their employers to stop**: Jamie Doward, "Attack on

Festive Hits 'Torture,'" *Guardian*, December 24, 2006, https://www.theguardian.com/uk/2006/dec/24/politics.musicnews.

34 **29 million new posts**: J. J. Pryor, "How Many Stories Are Published on Medium Each Month?" Medium, February 3, 2021, https://medium.com/feedium/how-many-stories-are-published-on-medium-each-month-fe4abb5c2ac0#:~:text=Well%2C%20for%20the%20quick%20answer,answer%20for%202020%20on%20Mr.

34 **four times as many**: "2021 Podcast Stats & Facts (New Research from APR 2021)," Podcast Insights, December 28, 2021, https://www.podcastinsights.com/podcast-statistics/#:~:text=Also%2C%20a%20common%20question%20is,episodes%20as%20of%20April%202021.

35 **500 hours of new video content**: Lori Lewis, "Infographic: What Happens in an Internet Minute 2021," All Access, https://www.allaccess.com/merge/archive/33341/infographic-what-happens-in-an-internet-minute.

35 **700,000 stories are posted on Instagram**: Werner Geyser, "TikTok Statistics—Revenue, Users & Engagement Stats (2022)," Influencer Marketing Hub, February 15, 2022, https://influencermarketinghub.com/tiktok-stats/.

35 **150,000 Slack messages**: "How Much Data Is Generated Every Minute on the Internet?," Daily Infographic, December 1, 2021, https://dailyinfographic.com/how-much-data-is-generated-every-minute.

35 **40,000 hours of music on Spotify**: Lewis, "Infographic."

35 **"Is that possible?"**: "Bo Burnham Inside: Can Anyone Shut Up Monologue," YouTube, https://www.youtube.com/watch?v=okq0hj1IMlo.

35 **one billion usage minutes**: Jacquelyn Bulao, "21 Impressive Slack Statistics You Must Know About in 2022," Techjury, May 2, 2022, https://techjury.net/blog/slack-statistics/#gref.

36 **4 hours and 23 minutes**: Scott Galloway, "In 2010, we spent

24 minutes on our phones," Twitter, January 25, 2022, https://twitter.com/profgalloway/status/1485965678683193349.

36 **850 minutes on the app**: Werner Geyser, "TikTok Statistics—Revenue, Users & Engagement Stats (2022)," Influencer Marketing Hub, February 15, 2022, https://influencermarketinghub.com/tiktok-stats/#toc-0.

36 **90 percent of us**: Nate Anderson, "88% of Americans Use a Second Screen While Watching TV. Why?," Ars Technica, December 26, 2019, https://arstechnica.com/gaming/2019/12/88-of-americans-use-a-second-screen-while-watching-tv-why/.

36 **Take your pick**: Christian P. Janssen et al., "Integrating Knowledge of Multitasking and Interruptions Across Different Perspectives and Research Methods," *International Journal of Human-Computer Studies* 79 (2015): 1–5, https://doi.org/10.1016/j.ijhcs.2015.03.002.

36 **40 percent of participants**: "Forget Your Kid's Phone Number? 'Digital Amnesia' Is Rampant, Poll Finds," CBC News, October 8, 2015, https://www.cbc.ca/news/science/digital-amnesia-kaspersky-1.3262600.

37 **twelve seconds to eight seconds**: Kevin McSpadden, "Science: You Now Have a Shorter Attention Span Than a Goldfish," *Time*, May 14, 2015, https://time.com/3858309/attention-spans-goldfish/.

38 ***Wired* predicted in 1999**: Kevin Kelly, "The Roaring Zeros," *Wired*, September 1, 1999, https://www.wired.com/1999/09/zeros/.

39 **"have literally rewired our brains"**: Aaron Holmes, "Facebook's Former Director of Monetization Says Facebook Intentionally Made Its Product as Addictive as Cigarettes—and Now He Fears It Could Cause 'Civil War,'" *Business Insider*, September 24, 2020, https://www.businessinsider.com/former-facebook-exec-addictive-as-cigarettes-tim-kendall-2020-9.

40 **450 selfies a year**: Sean Morrison, "Average Person Takes More Than 450 Selfies Every Year, Study Finds," *Evening Standard*, December 19, 2019, https://www.standard.co.uk/news/uk

/average-person-takes-more-than-450-selfies-every-year-study
-finds-a4317251.html.

40   **highest bid was $280**: Prabhat Verma, "They Spent a For-
tune on Pictures of Apes and Cats. Do They Regret It?," *Washington Post*, May 25, 2022, https://www.washingtonpost.com
/technology/2022/05/25/nft-value-drop/.

40   **Angry posts get shared**: "Most Influential Emotions on Social
Networks Revealed," *MIT Technology Review*, April 2, 2020,
https://www.technologyreview.com/2013/09/16/176450/most
-influential-emotions-on-social-networks-revealed/.

40   **more views than images**: "What Works on Tiktok: Our AI
Analysis," Butter Works, https://butter.works/clients/tiktok/
charts.

40   **are angrier than in the past**: Matt Labash, "High Steaks,"
blogpost, *Slack Tide by Matt Labash*, February 3, 2022, https:
//mattlabash.substack.com/p/high-steaks?s=r.

41   **five times as many**: "2021 Unruly Passenger Data," Federal Aviation Administration, March 1, 2022, https://www.faa.gov/data
_research/passengers_cargo/unruly_passengers/.

41   **Murder rates have soared**: Zusha Elinson, "Murders in U.S.
Cities Were Near Record Highs in 2021," *Wall Street Journal*, January 6, 2022, https://www.wsj.com/articles/murders-in-u-s-cities
-were-near-record-highs-in-2021-11641499978.

41   **contain tracking devices**: Simon Kuper, "The True Toll of the
Antivax Movement," *Financial Times*, January 13, 2022, https:
//www.ft.com/content/a1b5350a-4dba-40f4-833b-1e35199e2e9b.

42   **developed this disorder**: B. T. te Wildt et al., "Identität und
Dissoziation im Cyberspace," *Der Nervenarzt* 77, no. 1 (2006):
81–84, https://doi.org/10.1007/s00115-005-1893-x.

42   **often display dissociative symptoms**: Fatih Canan et al., "The
Association Between Internet Addiction and Dissociation Among
Turkish College Students," *Comprehensive Psychiatry* 53, no. 5
(2012): 422–26, https://doi.org/10.1016/j.comppsych.2011.08.006.

43   **obesity, type 2 diabetes**: Sami Ouanes and Julius Popp, "High
     Cortisol and the Risk of Dementia and Alzheimer's Disease: A
     Review of the Literature," *Frontiers in Aging Neuroscience* 11
     (2019), https://doi.org/10.3389/fnagi.2019.00043.

43   **"large doses of cortisol will kill you"**: Robert H. Lustig, *The
     Hacking of the American Mind: The Science Behind the Corpo-
     rate Takeover of Our Bodies and Brains* (New York: Avery, 2018):
     60–62.

43   **"poorer cognitive functioning . . . stupid things"**: Lustig
     quoted in Catherine Price, "Putting Down Your Phone May Help
     You Live Longer," *New York Times*, April 24, 2019, https://www
     .nytimes.com/2019/04/24/well/mind/putting-down-your-phone
     -may-help-you-live-longer.html.

43   **Cortisol can cause**: Terry Small, "Brain Bulletin #5—Stress
     Makes You Stupid," TerrySmall.com, https://www.terrysmall
     .com/blog/brain-bulletin-5-stress-makes-you-stupid#:~:text
     =When%20you%20stress%2C%20you%20release,for%20
     your%20brain%2C%20say%20researchers.

43   **"Your IQ plummets"**: Eric Hagerman, "Don't Panic—It
     Makes You Stupid," *Wired*, April 21 2008, https://www.wired
     .com/2008/04/gs-08dontpanic/.

44   **Facebook started losing**: Lexi Lonas, "Facebook Reports Los-
     ing Users for the First Time in Its History," *Hill*, February 4, 2022,
     https://thehill.com/policy/technology/592802-facebook-reports
     -losing-users-for-the-first-time-in-its-history/#:~:text=Facebook's
     %20earnings%20report%20on%20Wednesday,2021%2C%20the
     %20earnings%20report%20showed.

44   **Netflix lost subscribers**: Emma Roth, "Survey Shows Netflix Is
     Losing More Long-Term Subscribers," Verge, May 18, 2022, https:
     //www.theverge.com/2022/5/18/23125424/netflix-losing-long-term
     -subscribers-streaming.

45   **"Living amid the ever-rising waste"**: Ian Bogost, "People Aren't
     Meant to Talk This Much," *Atlantic*, February 16, 2022, https:

//www.theatlantic.com/technology/archive/2021/10/fix-facebook
-making-it-more-like-google/620456/.

3: STFU ON SOCIAL MEDIA

51 **Facebook, Instagram**: "Facebook: Daily Active Users Worldwide 2022," Statista, https://www.statista.com/statistics/346167
/facebook-global-dau/#:~:text=Facebook%20audience%20
reach&text=The%20number%20of%20monthly%20active,
from%2067.4%20percent%20in%202020.

51 **Instagram**: "Instagram Users Worldwide 2025," Statista, https:
//www.statista.com/statistics/183585/instagram-number-of-global
-users/.

51 **Snapchat**: "Snap Inc. Announces Fourth Quarter and Full Year
2021 Financial Results," Snap Inc., n.d., https://investor.snap.com
/news/news-details/2022/Snap-Inc.-Announces-Fourth-Quarter
-and-Full-Year-2021-Financial-Results/default.aspx.

51 **10 billion hours**: "Global Social Media Stats," DataReportal,
https://datareportal.com/social-media-users.

52 **60 percent of the time**: "CMU Researcher Seeks to Understand the Regret Behind Social Media," Human-Computer
Interaction Institute, n.d., https://www.hcii.cmu.edu/news/2021
/cmu-researcher-seeks-understand-regret-behind-social-media
#:~:text=At%20the%20end%20of%20the,in%20nearly%20
40%25%20of%20sessions.

52 **even more addictive**: Adi Robertson, "Social Media Harder
to Resist Than Cigarettes, According to Study," Verge, February 5,
2012, https://www.theverge.com/2012/2/5/2771255/social-media
-willpower-failure-chicago-university-study.

53 **company operates eighteen data centers**: Andrew Griffin, "Meta: Facebook Is Building 'the Most Powerful AI Computer in the World,'" *Independent*, January 24, 2022, https:
//www.independent.co.uk/tech/meta-facebook-ai-metaverse-rsc
-b1999605.html.

53 **two hundred Walmarts**: Rich Miller, "Facebook Has 47 Data Centers Under Construction," Data Center Frontier, November 10, 2021, https://datacenterfrontier.com/facebook-has-47-data -centers-under-construction/.

53 **344 times a day**: Trevor Wheelwright, "2022 Cell Phone Usage Statistics: How Obsessed Are We?," Reviews, January 24, 2022, https://www.reviews.org/mobile/cell-phone-addiction/#:~:text =using%20our%20phones%3F-,On%20average%2C%20Amer icans%20check%20their%20phones%20344%20times%20 per%20day,10%20minutes%20of%20waking%20up.

54 **they get more treats**: Bill Hathaway, "Likes and Shares Teach People to Express More Outrage Online," YaleNews, August 16, 2021, https://news.yale.edu/2021/08/13/likes-and-shares-teach -people-express-more-outrage-online.

54 **1.2 million tweets**: William J. Brady et al., "How Social Learning Amplifies Moral Outrage Expression in Online Social Networks," *Science Advances* 7, no. 33 (2021): https://doi.org/10 .1126/sciadv.abe5641.

54 **"create positive feedback loops"**: "Outrage Amplified," Findings, *Yale Alumni Magazine*, n.d., https://yalealumnimagazine .com/articles/5406-outrage-amplified.

54 **angrier in their personal lives**: Ryan C. Martin et al., "Anger on the Internet: The Perceived Value of Rant-Sites," *Cyberpsychology, Behavior, and Social Networking* 16, no. 2 (2013): https: //www.liebertpub.com/doi/10.1089/cyber.2012.0130.

54 **anger you experience online**: "Are Online Rants Good for Your Health?" Healthline, November 21, 2017, https://www .healthline.com/health-news/are-online-rants-good-for-your -health#Anger-is-the-real-problem.

55 **Each time your brain produces dopamine**: Anna Lembke, "Digital Addictions Are Drowning Us in Dopamine," *Wall Street Journal*, August 13, 2021, https://www.wsj.com/articles/digital -addictions-are-drowning-us-in-dopamine-11628861572.

56   **causes a sense of isolation**: Katherine Hobson, "Feeling Lonely? Too Much Time on Social Media May Be Why," NPR, March 6, 2017, https://www.npr.org/sections/health-shots/2017/03/06/518362255 /feeling-lonely-too-much-time-on-social-media-may-be-why.

57   **that we create "sacred spaces"**: Lauren Cassani Davis, "The Flight from Conversation," *Atlantic*, October 7, 2015, https: //www.theatlantic.com/technology/archive/2015/10/reclaiming -conversation-sherry-turkle/409273/.

57   **causes people to share less**: M. Lawton, "Reclaim Conversation from Technology, Suggests Clinical Psychologist," *Chicago Tribune*, May 23, 2019, https://www.chicagotribune.com /suburbs/lake-forest/ct-lfr-turkle-tl-1015–20151009-story.html.

57   **According to Emma Walker**: Bonnie Evie Gifford, "Our Digital Lives Are Overtaking Our Real-Life Interactions," *Happiful*, December 19, 2019, https://happiful.com/digital-conversations -overtake-real-life-interactions/.

57   **70 percent of women**: "Technoference: How Technology Can Hurt Relationships," Institute for Family Studies, n.d., https: //ifstudies.org/blog/technoference-how-technology-can-hurt -relationships#:~:text=62%25%20said%20technology%20 interferes%20with,the%20middle%20of%20a%20conversation.

57   **A 2021 study found**: Skye Bouffard, Deanna Giglio, and Zane Zheng, "Social Media and Romantic Relationship: Excessive Social Media Use Leads to Relationship Conflicts, Negative Outcomes, and Addiction via Mediated Pathways," *Social Science Computer Review*, https://doi.org/10.1177/08944393211013566.

57   **nearly 60 percent of people**: MediLexicon International, "How Does Social Media Affect Relationships?" Medical News Today, n.d., https://www.medicalnewstoday.com/articles/social -media-and-relationships#negative-effects.

57   **"has taught us to talk rather than listen"**: Kalev H. Leetaru, "Social Media Has Taught Us to Talk Rather Than Listen," *Forbes*, April 23, 2019, https://www.forbes.com/sites/kalevleetaru/2019

/04/23/social-media-has-taught-us-to-talk-rather-than-listen/?sh
=5783f5d155c0.

58 **80 percent of the time:** Lydia Dishman, "The Science of Why
We Talk Too Much (and How to Shut Up)," Fast Company, June
11, 2015, https://www.fastcompany.com/3047285/the-science-of
-why-we-talk-too-much-and-how-to-shut-up.

58 **70 percent say people on social media:** Amanda Lenhart,
"Teens, Technology, and Friendships," Pew Research Center: Internet, Science and Tech, May 30, 2020, https://www.pewresearch
.org/internet/2015/08/06/teens-technology-and-friendships/.

58 **might even improve relationships:** M. E. Morris, "Enhanc-
ing Relationships Through Technology: Directions in Parenting,
Caregiving, Romantic Partnerships, and Clinical Practice," *Dia-
logues in Clinical Neuroscience* 22, no. 2 (2020): 151–60, https:
//doi.org/10.31887/dcns.2020.22.2/mmorris.

59 **"Are There Any Adults":** Josh Barro, "Are There Any Adults
at the Washington Post?" June 7, 2022, https://www.joshbarro
.com/p/are-there-any-adults-at-the-washington?utm_source
=email&s=r.

59 **social media they later regretted:** Sarah Snow, "Don't Post
That! Why Half of Americans Regret Their Social Media Posts,"
Social Media Today, July 28, 2015, https://www.socialmediatoday
.com/news/dont-post-that-why-half-of-americans-regret-their
-social-media-posts/454600/.

60 **YouGov America survey:** Jake Gammon, "Social Media Blun-
ders Cause More Damage to Important Relationships Today Than
Two Years Ago," YouGovAmerica, July 22, 2015, https://today
.yougov.com/topics/lifestyle/articles-reports/2015/07/22/social
-media-blunders-cause-more-damage-important-.

60 **she found comments from:** Yang Wang et al., "I Regretted the
Minute I Pressed Share: A Qualitative Study of Regrets on Facebook,"
Carnegie Mellon University, n.d., https://cups.cs.cmu.edu/soups/2011
/proceedings/a10_Wang.pdf.

60 posted something they later regretted: "Many Young Amer-
    icans Regret Online Posts Made While High," MedicineNet,
    August 7, 2019, https://www.medicinenet.com/script/main/art
    .asp?articlekey=223426.

61 The   thirty-nine-year-old: "Calvin   Newport—Georgetown
    University," n.d., https://people.cs.georgetown.edu/~cnewport/.

62 limits his Instagram use: "Comedian on Being Kicked Off
    Stage," YouTube, December 19, 2019, https://www.youtube.com
    /watch?v=3n9CsdcLP4g.

62 "mindful scrolling": Arthur C. Brooks, "How to Break a Phone
    Addiction," Atlantic, October 7, 2021, https://www.theatlantic.com
    /family/archive/2021/10/digital-addiction-smartphone/620318/.

4: MANSPLAINING, MANTERRUPTING, AND MANALOGUES

66 two out of five women: Allison Sadlier, "This Is How Often
    Women in the US Experience Mansplaining," New York Post,
    March 16, 2020, https://nypost.com/2020/03/16/this-is-how-often
    -women-in-the-us-experience-mansplaining/.

66 you practice saying: Soraya Chemaly, "10 Simple Words
    Every Girl Should Learn," Role Reboot, May 6, 2014, http://www
    .rolereboot.org/culture-and-politics/details/2014–05–10-simple
    -words-every-girl-learn/.

67 Apparently, she got the numbers: Tracy Clark-Flory, "Fact-
    Checking 'the Female Brain,'" Salon, September 25, 2011, https:
    //www.salon.com/2006/09/26/gender_difference_2/.

67 "A stereotype always has": Deborah Solomon, "He Thought,
    She Thought: Questions for Dr. Louann Brizendine," New York
    Times, December 10, 2006, https://www.nytimes.com/2006/12
    /10/magazine/10wwln_q4.html.

67 later editions of her book: Stephen Moss, "Do Women
    Really Talk More?," Guardian, November 27, 2006, https://www
    .theguardian.com/lifeandstyle/2006/nov/27/familyandrelationships.

69 **"Women in tech"**: Kieran Snyder, "How to Get Ahead as a Woman in Tech: Interrupt Men," *Slate*, July 23, 2014, https://slate .com/human-interest/2014/07/study-men-interrupt-women-more -in-tech-workplaces-but-high-ranking-women-learn-to-interrupt .html.

70 **They are more likely to speak**: Elizabeth Redden, "Study: Men Speak 1.6 Times More Than Women in College Classrooms," *Inside Higher Ed*, https://www.insidehighered.com/quicktakes/2021/01 /19/study-men-speak-16-times-more-women-college-classrooms.

70 **according to a 2017 study**: Colleen Flaherty, "The Missing Women," Inside Higher Ed's News, *Inside Higher Ed*, https: //www.insidehighered.com/news/2017/12/19/study-finds-men -speak-twice-often-do-women-colloquiums.

70 **teachers perceive girls as more talkative**: Marina Bassi et al., "Failing to Notice? Uneven Teachers' Attention to Boys and Girls in the Classroom," *IZA Journal of Labor Economics* 7, no. 9 (2018), https://izajole.springeropen.com/articles/10.1186/s40172 -018-0069-4.

70 **the men considered the discussion**: Bernice Ng, "Are Male-Dominated Workspaces Harmful to Women?," *Marie France Asia*, May 20, 2016, https://www.mariefranceasia.com/career -advice/tips-for-success/male-dominated-workspaces-harmful -women-123584.html.

70 **Spender's famous quote**: "Language Myth # 6," Language as Prejudice, Do You Speak American?, PBS, https://www.pbs.org /speak/speech/prejudice/women/.

70 **there were forty-eight interruptions**: Don Zimmerman and Candace West, "Sex Roles, Interruptions, and Silence in Conversation," Stanford University, https://www.web.stanford.edu /~eckert/PDF/zimmermanwest1975.pdf.

71 **Researchers at George Washington**: Adrienne B. Hancock and Benjamin A. Rubin, "Influence of Communication Partner's Gender

on Language," *Journal of Language and Social Psychology* 34, no. 1 (2014): 46–64, https://doi.org/10.1177/0261927x14533197.

71   **Professors at the Northwestern Pritzker**: J. Carlisle Larsen, "Study Shows Female Supreme Court Justices Get Interrupted More Often Than Male Colleagues," Wisconsin Public Radio, April 19, 2019, https://www.wpr.org/study-shows-female-supreme-court-justices-get-interrupted-more-often-male-colleagues.

71   **started calling on women**: Juliet Eilperin, "White House Women Want to Be in the Room Where It Happens," *Washington Post*, October 28, 2021, https://www.washingtonpost.com/news/powerpost/wp/2016/09/13/white-house-women-are-now-in-the-room-where-it-happens/.

72   **Tannen wrote in *Harvard Business Review***: Deborah Tannen, "The Power of Talk: Who Gets Heard and Why," *Harvard Business Review*, October 15, 2019, https://hbr.org/1995/09/the-power-of-talk-who-gets-heard-and-why.

72   **Men predicted the same grades**: Laurie Heatherington et al., "Two Investigations of Female Modesty in Achievement Situations," *Sex Roles* 29, no. 11–12 (1993): 739–54, https://doi.org/10.1007/bf00289215.

72   **John Gray, author of *Men Are from Mars***: Susan Adams, "8 Blind Spots Between the Sexes at Work," *Forbes*, April 26, 2013, https://www.forbes.com/sites/susanadams/2013/04/26/8-blind-spots-between-the-sexes-at-work/?sh=3cfec433314d.

72   **Men also are more prone**: Rob Kendall, "5 Ways Men and Women Talk Differently," *Psychology Today*, December 15, 2016, https://www.psychologytoday.com/us/blog/blamestorming/201612/5-ways-men-and-women-talk-differently.

73   **example of unconscious bias toward women**: Charlotte Alter, "Google's Eric Schmidt Called Out for Interrupting the Only Woman on the Panel," *Time*, March 17, 2015, https://time.com/3748208/google-exec-eric-schmidt-called-out-for-interrupting-only-woman-on-panel/.

73 **Trans men are interrupted**: Jessica Nordell, "Why Aren't Women Advancing at Work? Ask a Transgender Person," *New Republic*, August 27, 2014, https://newrepublic.com/article/119239 /transgender-people-can-explain-why-women-dont-advance -work.

74 **"Ben has migrated"**: Shankar Vedantam, "How the Sex Bias Prevails," Age, May 14, 2010, https://www.theage.com .au/national/how-the-sex-bias-prevails-20100514-v4mv.html #ixzz3BXBN2SNG.

74 **"because society has accepted"**: Jason Maderer, "Women Interrupted: A New Strategy for Male-Dominated Discussions," News, Carnegie Mellon University, October 20, 2021, https: //www.cmu.edu/news/stories/archives/2020/october/women -interrupted-debate.html.

76 **former Facebook chief operating officer**: Sheryl Sandberg and Adam Grant, "Speaking While Female," *New York Times*, January 12, 2015, https://www.nytimes.com/2015/01/11/opinion /sunday/speaking-while-female.html.

77 **Over time, women justices**: Larsen, "Study Shows Female Supreme Court Justices Get Interrupted More Often Than Male Colleagues."

5: STFU AS MEDICINE

83 **Many docs say this is complete quackery**: Louise Tickle, "Positive Thinking Can Kill Cancer Cells, Say Psychologists," *Guardian*, April 16, 2000, https://www.theguardian.com/uk/2000 /apr/16/theobserver.uknews2.

87 **up to 2,000 times a day**: Alexis Blue, "Frequent 'I-Talk' May Signal Proneness to Emotional Distress," University of Arizona News, March 7, 2018, https://news.arizona.edu/story/frequent -italk-may-signal-proneness-emotional-distress.

87 **A Harvard study found**: Erik C. Nook et al., "Linguistic Measures of Psychological Distance Track Symptom Levels and

Treatment Outcomes in a Large Set of Psychotherapy Transcripts," *Proceedings of the National Academy of Sciences* 119, no. 13 (2022), https://doi.org/10.1073/pnas.2114737119.

88 **Researchers at the University of Michigan**: Ariana Orvell et al., "Does Distanced Self-Talk Facilitate Emotion Regulation Across a Range of Emotionally Intense Experiences?," *Clinical Psychological Science* 9, no. 1 (2020), 68–78, https://doi.org/10.1177 /2167702620951539.

89 **website for the Japan National Tourism Organization**: Japan National Tourism Organization, "Forest Bathing in Japan (Shinrin-Yoku)," Travel Japan, https://www.japan.travel/en/guide/forest -bathing/.

89 **forests of the Kii Peninsula**: "Sacred Sites & Pilgrimage Routes in the Kii Mountain Range (UNESCO): World Heritage," Travel Japan, https://www.japan.travel/en/world-heritage/sacred-sites-and-pilgrimage-routes-in-the-kii-mountain-range/.

90 **One Japanese study**: Akemi Furuyashiki et al., "A Comparative Study of the Physiological and Psychological Effects of Forest Bathing (Shinrin-Yoku) on Working Age People with and without Depressive Tendencies," *Environmental Health and Preventive Medicine* 24, no. 1 (2019), https://doi.org/10.1186/s12199-019 -0800-1.

91 **jibe with other research**: Kirste et al., "Is Silence Golden?," 1221–28.

91 **"neurogenesis" creates greater resiliency**: Ruth Williams, "Young Brain Cells Silence Old Ones to Quash Anxiety," *Scientist Magazine*, June 27, 2019, https://www.the-scientist.com/news -opinion/young-brain-cells-silence-old-ones-to-quash-anxiety -64385.

92 **"well-being forest trail"**: Eira-Maija Savonen, "Forest Therapy and the Health Benefits of Forest," February 27, 2019, https://www.vomentaga.ee/sites/default/files/editor/failid/forest

_therapy_and_the_health_benefits_of_forest_karvia_27.2.2019
_moniste_jaettavaksi.pdf.

92   **so-called power forests**: "Forest Bathing," Alpenwelt Resort,
      https://www.alpenwelt.net/en/summer-autumn-holiday/forest
      -bathing/.

96   **Buddhist monks and nuns**: Gauri Verma and Ricardo Araya,
      "The Effect of Meditation on Psychological Distress Among Bud-
      dhist Monks and Nuns," *International Journal of Psychiatry in
      Medicine* 40, no. 4 (2010): 461–68, https://doi.org/10.2190/pm
      .40.4.h.

96   **change the structure of your brain**: Eileen Luders, Nicolas
      Cherbuin, and Florian Kurth, "Forever Young(er): Potential Age-
      Defying Effects of Long-Term Meditation on Gray Matter Atro-
      phy," *Frontiers in Psychology* 5 (2015), https://doi.org/10.3389
      /fpsyg.2014.01551.

96   **doctors at Johns Hopkins reported**: Madhav Goyal et al.,
      "Meditation Programs for Psychological Stress and Well-Being,"
      JAMA Internal Medicine 174, no. 3 (2014): 357, https://doi.org/10
      .1001/jamainternmed.2013.13018.

96   **gives your brain a workout**: Randy L. Buckner, "The Brain's
      Default Network: Origins and Implications for the Study of Psy-
      chosis," *Dialogues in Clinical Neuroscience* 15, no. 3 (2013): 351–
      58, https://doi.org/10.31887/dcns.2013.15.3/rbuckner.

97   **can't last the full ten days**: Marcus Baram, "Silent Mode:
      Why the Stars of Silicon Valley Are Turning to Silent Medita-
      tion Retreats," Fast Company, April 12, 2019, https://www.fast
      company.com/90334124/from-hacking-the-mind-to-punishing
      -ennui-techs-brightest-are-taking-to-silent-retreats.

97   **meditation apps have become a billion-dollar business**: "How
      Meditation Apps Became a Billion-Dollar Industry," Newsy, May
      2, 2022, https://www.newsy.com/stories/how-meditation-apps
      -became-a-billion-dollar-industry/.

97 **2,500 of them have been released**: Jazmin Goodwin, "Health and Wellness Apps Offer Free Services to Help Those Coping with Coronavirus," *USA Today*, March 25, 2020, https://www .usatoday.com/story/tech/2020/03/21/health-and-wellness-apps -offer-freebies-coping-coronavirus/2892085001/.

6: STFU AT WORK

102 **bills itself as**: Derek du Preez, "GE Staying Current by Becoming an 'As-a-Service' Business," *Diginomica*, April 29, 2019, https://diginomica.com/ge-staying-current-by-becoming-an -as-a-service-business.

102 **Hal Gregersen**: Hal Gregersen, "Bursting Out of the CEO Bubble," *Harvard Business Review*, February 21, 2017, https: //hbr.org/2017/03/bursting-the-ceo-bubble.

102 **four minutes out of every twenty-four:** The 4-24 Project, https:// 4-24project.org/.

104 **plowing that budget into research**: Steven Loveday, "Tesla Spends Least on Ads, Most on R&D: Report," InsideEVs, March 25, 2022, https://insideevs.com/news/575848/tesla-highest -research-development-no-ads/.

104 **got rid of his public relations team**: Fred Lambert, "Tesla Dissolves Its PR Department—A New First in the Industry," Electrek, October 6, 2020, https://electrek.co/2020/10/06/tesla -dissolves-pr-department/.

105 **engineer at one of Musk's other companies**: C. W. Headley, "Steve Jobs Once Did This for 20 Seconds and It Became a Leg- endary Power Move," Ladders, December 14, 2020, https://www .theladders.com/career-advice/steve-jobs-once-did-this-for-20 -seconds-and-it-became-a-legendary-power-move.

106 **call starts to feel like an interrogation:** Chris Orlob, "This Is What a 'Deal Closing' Discovery Call Looks Like," Gong, July 5, 2017, https://www.gong.io/blog/deal-closing-discovery-call/.

106 **spend forty-three days:** "Hold Up—More than 80 Percent of

People Are Put on Hold Every Time They Contact a Business," Talkto, Cision PR Newswire, January 23, 2013, https://www .prnewswire.com/news-releases/hold-up—more-than-80-percent -of-people-are-put-on-hold-every-time-they-contact-a-business -188032061.html.

107 **knowing how to control your own emotions**: Myra Bry-ant Golden, "Customer Service: Call Control Strategies," video tutorial, LinkedIn, August 14, 2019, https://www.linkedin.com /learning/customer-service-call-control-strategies/give-a-limited -response?autoplay=true&resume=false.

113 **Axsom's paper**: Jason R. Axsom, "Compulsive Talkers: Per-ceptions of Over Talkers Within the Workplace" master's thesis, University of Nebraska at Omaha, 2006, https://digitalcommons .unomaha.edu/studentwork/205/.

115 **39 percent of people**: "You Waste a Lot of Time at Work," Atlassian, n.d., https://www.atlassian.com/time-wasting-at-work -infographic.

115 **8 to 10 percent each year**: "Minutes (Wasted) of Meeting: 50 Shocking Meeting Statistics," *BOOQED* (blog), n.d., https://www .booqed.com/blog/minutes-wasted-of-meeting-50-shocking -meeting-statistics.

115 **averaging 44.6 hours a week**: "Productivity Trends Report: One-on-One Meeting Statistics: Reclaim," RSS, n.d., https: //reclaim.ai/blog/productivity-report-one-on-one-meetings.

116 **resist the urge**: Gino Spocchia, "'Walk Out of a Meeting': Elon Musk's Six Rules for Staff Resurfaces," Yahoo! News, April 28, 2021, https://money.yahoo.com/walk-meeting-elon-musk-six-154936765 .html.

116 **91 percent of people**: Flynn, "27 Incredible Meeting Statistics."

117 **most common complaint**: Flynn, "27 Incredible Meeting Sta-tistics."

118 **two-thirds of conversations**: Adam M. Mastroianni et al., "Do Conversations End When People Want Them To?" *Proceedings of*

the National Academy of Sciences 118, no. 10 (2021), https://doi .org/10.1073/pnas.2011809118.

122 **Another got twenty-two**: "Constellation Research," You-Tube, https://www.youtube.com/c/ConstellationResearch/videos.

122 **75 percent less stress**: Brian O'Connell, "Hail to the 'Humble' Manager," SHRM, July 6, 2021, https://www.shrm.org /resourcesandtools/hr-topics/people-managers/pages/managing -with-humility-.aspx.

123 **global luxury hospitality chain**: Sue Shellenbarger, "The Best Bosses Are Humble Bosses," *Wall Street Journal*, October 9, 2018, https://www.wsj.com/articles/the-best-bosses-are-humble-bosses -1539092123.

7: STFU AT HOME

129 **it gained widespread use only in the 1970s**: Alison Gopnik, "A Manifesto Against 'Parenting,'" *Wall Street Journal*, July 8, 2016, https://www.wsj.com/articles/a-manifesto-against-parenting -1467991745.

129 **terrified that our kids**: Claire Cain Miller, "The Relentlessness of Modern Parenting," *New York Times*, December 25, 2018, https://www.nytimes.com/2018/12/25/upshot/the-relentlessness -of-modern-parenting.html.

129 **"reduced children's playtime"**: K. H. Kim, "The Creativity Crisis: It's Getting Worse," Idea to Value, n.d., https://www.ideatovalue .com/crea/khkim/2017/04/creativity-crisis-getting-worse/.

130 **feed them constant praise**: Michaeleen Doucleff, "How to Be a Calmer Parent and Stop Arguing with Your Kids," *Time*, March 6, 2021, https://time.com/5944210/calm-parenting-technique/.

130 **Hunter, Gather, Parent**: Michaeleen Doucleff, *Hunter, Gather, Parent: What Ancient Cultures Can Teach Us About the Lost Art of Raising Happy, Helpful Little Humans* (New York: Avid Reader Press, 2021), 127.

130 **Duct Tape Parenting**: Vicki Hoefle, *Duct Tape Parenting: A*

Less Is More Approach to Raising Respectful, Responsible, and Resilient Kids (New York, NY: Bibliomotion, 2012).

131 **"the excercise can be transforming"**: Mary Dickinson Bird, "Talk More, Say Less," *Science and Children* 38, no. 4 (2001): 47–50.

132 **how to be innovative**: Allison Gopnik, *The Gardener and the Carpenter: What the New Science of Child Development Tells Us About the Relationship Between Parents and Children* (New York: St. Martin's Press, 2017).

132 **"silence in a noisy world"**: Maxwell King, *The Good Neighbor: The Life and Work of Fred Rogers* (New York: Abrams Press, 2018).

132 **Mary McNamara wrote in the *Los Angeles Times***: Mary McNamara, "'A Beautiful Day' Is a Great Movie. It Just Misses the Point of Mister Rogers," *Los Angeles Times*, November 30, 2019, https://www.latimes.com/entertainment-arts/story /2019–11–30/beautiful-day-neighborhood-is-a-great-movie-its -just-not-about-mister-rogers.

133 **Silence, done well**: "Fred Rogers Acceptance Speech—1997," YouTube, n.d., https://www.youtube.com/watch?v=Upm9Lnu CBUM.

134 ***The Self-Driven Child***: William Stixrud and Ned Johnson, *The Self-Driven Child: The Science and Sense of Giving Your Kids More Control over Their Lives* (New York: Penguin Books, 2019).

134 **Tavenner encourages parents**: Diane Tavenner, "How I Learned to Let My Kid Fail," *Time*, September 26, 2019, https: //time.com/5687129/children-failure/.

135 **Michelle Obama says that's the best gift**: Maija Kappler, "9 Parenting Tips from Michelle Obama and Her Mom," *HuffPost*, September 17, 2020, https://www.huffpost.com/archive/ca/entry /michelle-obama-parenting-tips_ca_5f623cc8c5b61845586574e6.

135 **"That was the gift"**: Róisín Ingle, "Michelle Obama: World's Most Powerful People 'Aren't That Smart,'" *Irish Times*,

December 4, 2018, https://www.irishtimes.com/culture/books
/michelle-obama-world-s-most-powerful-people-aren-t-that
-smart-1.3719527.

136 **"Motherhood has taught me"**: H.R.H. the Duchess of Sussex,
"HRH the Duchess of Sussex Interviews Michelle Obama in the
September Issue," British *Vogue*, July 29, 2019, https://www.vogue
.co.uk/article/michelle-obama-duchess-of-sussex-interview-2019.

136 **"There is nothing better"**: Michael Hainey, "Lin-Manuel
Miranda Thinks the Key to Parenting Is a Little Less Parenting,"
GQ, April 26, 2016, https://www.gq.com/story/unexpected-lin
-manuel-miranda.

136 **A lot of new research shows**: Pamela Paul, "Let Children Get
Bored Again," *New York Times*, February 2, 2019, https://www
.nytimes.com/2019/02/02/opinion/sunday/children-bored.html.

137 **Belton says kids need**: Hannah Richardson, "Children Should
Be Allowed to Get Bored, Expert Says," BBC News, March 23,
2013, https://www.bbc.com/news/education-21895704.

137 **people who performed a boring task**: Sandi Mann and Rebekah
Cadman, "Does Being Bored Make Us More Creative?" *Creativity Research Journal* 26, no. 2 (2014): 165–73, https://doi.org/10
.1080/10400419.2014.901073.

137 **Aaron Sorkin gets so many great ideas**: Tat Bellamy-Walker,
"A Former Twitter Exec Reveals the Simple Strategy Used by
Jack Dorsey and Steve Jobs That Helped His Team Be More Creative at Work," *Business Insider*, August 14, 2020, https://www
.businessinsider.com/how-to-be-creative-twitter-apple-aaron
-sorkin-innovative-distraction.

138 **Queen wasn't a very good mother**: Becky Pemberton, "Lonely
Prince: How Charles Felt the Queen Was a 'Cold and Distant'
Mother," *U.S. Sun*, December 17, 2019, https://www.the-sun.com
/lifestyle/165255/how-charles-felt-the-queen-was-a-cold-and
-distant-mother-but-she-didnt-want-to-burden-him-with-duties
-as-a-boy/.

138 *The Palace Papers*: Sam Knight, "The Collateral Damage of Queen Elizabeth's Glorious Reign," *New Yorker*, April 29, 2022, https://www.newyorker.com/news/letter-from-the-uk/the-collateral-damage-of-queen-elizabeths-glorious-reign.

138 **Charles has been derided in the British press**: Zoë Heller, "Where Prince Charles Went Wrong," *New Yorker*, April 3, 2017, https://www.newyorker.com/magazine/2017/04/10/where-prince-charles-went-wrong.

138 **a "prat," a "twit," and an "idiot"**: Jamie Grierson, "Publication of Prince Charles 'Black Spider' Letters: Live," *Guardian*, May 13, 2015, https://www.theguardian.com/uk-news/live/2015/may/13/publication-of-the-prince-charles-black-spider-letters-live.

139 **The Queen did her job**: Zoe Forsey, "Queen's Furious Letter to Princess Diana That Finally Ended Marriage to Charles," *Daily Mirror*, April 30, 2020, https://www.mirror.co.uk/news/uk-news/queens-furious-letter-princess-diana-21491557.

139 **she gave an emotionless three-minute live address**: Forsey, "Queen's Furious Letter to Princess Diana That Finally Ended Marriage to Charles."

140 **"Give TV interviews by all means"**: Kenneth Garger, "What Prince Philip Thought of Harry and Meghan's Oprah Interview," Page Six, April 12, 2020, https://pagesix.com/2021/04/11/prince-philip-thought-harry-and-meghan-markles-interview-was-madness/.

140 **"the 'stiff upper lip'"**: François Marmouvet, "In Defence of the British Stiff Upper Lip," Conversation, November 16, 2021, https://theconversation.com/in-defence-of-the-british-stiff-upper-lip-77347.

140 **Finland was named the happiest country**: Vicky McKeever, "This Country Has Been Named the World's Happiest for the Fifth Year in a Row," CNBC, March 18, 2022, https://www.cnbc.com/2022/03/18/finland-named-the-worlds-happiest-for-the-fifth-year-in-a-row.html.

141 **"Silence is gold"**: Laura Studarus, "How the Finnish Survive Without Small Talk," BBC Travel, October 18, 2018, https://www.bbc.com/travel/article/20181016-how-the-finnish-survive-without-small-talk.

141 **"Why can't we stick to our usual four meters?"**: "What Makes a Happy Country?," *Indian Express*, April 26, 2021, https://indianexpress.com/article/world/what-makes-a-happy-country-7289534/.

141 **"silence travel"**: Aleksi Teivainen, "Silence an Opportunity for Finnish Tourism Industry," *Helsinki Times*, September 4, 2014, https://www.helsinkitimes.fi/business/11886-silence-an-opportunity-for-finnish-tourism-industry.html.

141 **"Looking for a place so quiet"**: "8 Ways to Enjoy the Silence: Visit Finnish Lapland," Lapland Above Ordinary, January 12, 2022, https://www.lapland.fi/visit/only-in-lapland/8-ways-enjoy-silence-remote-holiday-destination/.

141 **When he retired**: Subham Jindal, "'I Will Miss the Silence': Sebastian Vettel Pays a Heartfelt Tribute to Former Ferrari Teammate Kimi Raikkonen," SportsRush, December 1, 2021, https://thesportsrush.com/f1-news-i-will-miss-the-silence-sebastian-vettel-pays-a-heartfelt-tribute-to-former-ferrari-teammate-kimi-raikkonen/.

141 **Räikkönen said he might consent**: Aditya Talpade, "'Only Silent Films': Oscar Winner Travon Free Describes Conversation About Movies with Kimi Räikkönen," Sportskeeda, December 2, 2021, https://www.sportskeeda.com/f1/news-oscar-winner-travon-free-describes-conversation-movies-kimi-raikkonen.

141 **No standardized tests**: Mike Colagrossi, "10 Reasons Why Finland's Education System Is the Best in the World," World Economic Forum, September 10, 2018, https://www.weforum.org/agenda/2018/09/10-reasons-why-finlands-education-system-is-the-best-in-the-world.

141 **Kids start school at a later age**: LynNell Hancock, "Why Are Finland's Schools Successful?," *Smithsonian Magazine*, https://www.smithsonianmag.com/innovation/why-are-finlands-schools-successful-49859555/#:~:text=Ninety%2Dthree%20percent%20of%20Finns,student%20than%20the%20United%20States.

142 **do their homework on their own**: "Natural Parenting in Finland: Raising Kids Who Love to Learn," Friso, n.d., https://www.friso.com.sg/guides/natural-parenting-finland-raising-kids-who-love-learn#:~:text=The%20Finnish%20believe%20that%20play,their%20preferences%20in%20the%20process.

142 **Finnish families build backyard play huts**: Seiko Mochida, "Home Visit Survey in Finland: Children Playing Cheerfully and Freely—A Work-Life Balance to Support Childrearing by Parents—Current Situation Regarding Children's "Attitudes of Learning to Learn," Child Research Net, September 29, 2017, https://www.childresearch.net/projects/ecec/2017_14.html.

143 **"reading between the lines"**: "Chinmoku, Sontaku and the Uses of Silence," Japanology, April 1, 2019, https://japanology.org/2019/03/chinmoku-sontaku-and-the-uses-of-silence/.

143 **masters of quiet parenting**: Mrs. H., "Parenting in Public: 10 Hidden Rules Among Japanese Parents to Follow When in Japan," Tsunagu Japan, n.d., https://www.tsunagujapan.com/10-unwritten-social-rules-of-japanese-parenting/.

144 **"I began noticing this everywhere"**: Kate Lewis, "The Japanese Way of Disciplining Children," Savvy Tokyo, February 17, 2021, https://savvytokyo.com/japanese-way-disciplining-children/.

144 **United Nations' annual World Happiness Report**: Genkidesu, "The World Happiness Report 2020: How Happy Is Japan?," City-Cost, June 30, 2020, https://www.city-cost.com/blogs/CityCostInsiders/z42mk-living.

144 **Japanese value quieter things:** Genkidesu, "The World Happiness Report 2020: How Happy Is Japan?"

144 **according to Héctor García**: Héctor García and Francesc Miralles, *Ikigai: The Japanese Secret to a Long and Happy Life* (New York: Penguin Books, 2017).

8: STFU IN LOVE

147 **environmentalist named John Francis**: "How Do Years of Silence Change Someone?" NPR, November 21, 2014, https://www.npr.org/2014/11/21/364150411/how-do-years-of-silence-change-someone.

148 **couples need to learn how to have a fight**: Gary W. Lewandowski, "Most Couples Need to Fight More, Not Less—Here's Why and How to Do It," IDEAS.TED.com, April 15, 2021, https://ideas.ted.com/most-couples-need-to-be-fighting-more-not-less-heres-why-and-how-to-do-it/.

149 **half of married couples**: "Does Marriage Counseling Work? Your Questions Answered," OpenCounseling, May 18, 2022, https://www.opencounseling.com/blog/does-marriage-counseling-work-your-questions-answered.

149 **Second and third marriages**: "Divorce Statistics and Facts: What Affects Divorce Rates in the U.S.?," Wilkinson and Finkbeiner, March 3, 2022, https://www.wf-lawyers.com/divorce-statistics-and.

149 **Twenty-five percent of couples**: Susan Gilbert, "Married with Problems? Therapy May Not Help," *New York Times*, April 19, 2005, https://www.nytimes.com/2005/04/19/health/psychology/married-with-problems-therapy-may-not-help.html.

149 **"How Therapy Can Be Hazardous"**: William Doherty, "Bad Couples Therapy," Psychotherapy Networker, December 30, 2008, https://www.psychotherapynetworker.org/blog/details/369/bad-couples-therapy.

149 **University of Groningen in the Netherlands**: Namkje Koudenburg, Ernestine H. Gordijn, and Tom Postmes, "'More Than Words': Social Validation in Close Relationships," *Personality and*

Social Psychology Bulletin 40, no. 11 (2014): 1517–28, https://doi .org/10.1177/0146167214549945.

149 **advises clients to carve out**: Suzanne B. Phillips, "Post: Understanding the Sounds of Silence in Your Relationship," Couples After Trauma, February 5, 2010, https://couplesaftertrauma.com/2010 /02/05/understanding-the-sounds-of-silence-in-your-relationship/.

150 **professor at the State University**: Arthur Aron et al., "The Experimental Generation of Interpersonal Closeness: A Procedure and Some Preliminary Findings," *Personality and Social Psychology Bulletin* 23, no. 4 (1997): 363–77, https://doi.org/10.1177 /0146167297234003.

150 **most important thing you will ever do**: UC Berkeley Campus Life, "The Science of Love with Arthur Aron," YouTube, February 12, 2015, https://www.youtube.com/watch?v=gVff7TjzF3A.

151 **"relationship closeness induction task"**: Constantine Sedikides, "The Relationship Closeness Induction Task," *Representative Research in Social Psychology* 23 (1999): 1–4, https://www .psychology.uga.edu/sites/default/files/RCITarticle1999.pdf.

151 *How to Fall in Love with Anyone*: Mandy Len Catron, *How to Fall in Love with Anyone: A Memoir in Essays* (New York: Simon and Schuster, 2018).

151 **describes in her *New York Times* article**: Mandy Len Catron, "To Fall in Love with Anyone, Do This," *New York Times*, January 9, 2015, https://www.nytimes.com/2015/01/11/style/modern -love-to-fall-in-love-with-anyone-do-this.html.

151 **results, shown in a five-minute video**: Upworthy, "How Would You React After Looking in the Eyes of a War Refugee?," YouTube, https://www.youtube.com/watch?v=By_BHbskg_E&t=237s.

151 **"Four minutes of eye contact"**: Parker Molloy, "4 Minutes of Silence Can Boost Your Empathy for Others. Watch as Refugees Try It Out," Upworthy, October 21, 2021, https://www.upworthy .com/4-minutes-of-silence-can-boost-your-empathy-for-others -watch-as-refugees-try-it-out.

153 **"TALK," short for "Topic selection, Asking questions"**: Alison Wood Brooks, Faculty and Research, Harvard Business School, https://www.hbs.edu/faculty/Pages/profile.aspx?facId=684820.

154 *Harvard Business Review* **article**: Alison Wood Brooks and Leslie K. John, "The Surprising Power of Questions," *Harvard Business Review*, May–June 2018, https://hbr.org/2018/05/the -surprising-power-of-questions.

155 **38 percent and 55 percent**: "How to Use the 7–38–55 Rule to Negotiate Effectively," MasterClass, https://www.masterclass .com/articles/how-to-use-the-7–38–55-rule-to-negotiate -effectively#how-to-use-the-73855-rule-to-negotiate-effectively.

155 **1971 book,** *Silent Messages*: Albert Mehrabian, *Silent Messages* (Belmont, California: Wadsworth Publishing, 1971).

155 **Mehrabian himself has claimed**: "Albert Mehrabian," British Library, n.d., https://www.bl.uk/people/albert-mehrabian#:~:text =Drawing%20on%20the%20combined%20findings,liking%20 %2B%2055%25%20facial%20liking.

156 **based on the way they talked to each other**: "John Gottman," Wikipedia, https://en.wikipedia.org/wiki/John_Gottman#The _Gottman_Method_of_Relationship_Therapy.

156 **predicted which couples he believed would break up**: K. T. Buehlman, J. M. Gottman, and L. F. Katz, "How a Couple Views Their Past and Predicts Their Future: Predicting Divorce from an Oral History Interview," *Journal of Family Psychology* 5, nos. 3–4 (1992): 295–318, https://doi.org/10.1037/0893–3200.5.3–4.295.

157 **Gottman has authored**: "A Research-Based Approach to Relationships," Gottman Institute, May 19, 2022, https://www.gottman .com/.

157 **better state of mind**: Ellie Lisitsa, "The Four Horsemen: Criticism, Contempt, Defensiveness, and Stonewalling," Gottman Institute, May 11, 2022, https://www.gottman.com/blog/the-four -horsemen-recognizing-criticism-contempt-defensiveness-and -stonewalling/.

158 **conversation with sarcasm or negativity:** Joseph Klemz, "How Dr. Gottman Can Predict Divorce with 94% Accuracy," Real Life Counseling, July 31, 2018, https://reallifecounseling.us /predict-divorce-gottman/#:~:text=One%20of%20the%20rea sons%20Dr,makes%20at%20de%2Descalating%20tension.

158 **Gottman Institute advises:** Kyle Benson, "5 Steps to Fight Better If Your Relationship Is Worth Fighting For," Gottman Institute, February 3, 2021, https://www.gottman.com/blog/5 -steps-to-fight-better-if-your-relationship-is-worth-fighting-for/.

158 **Jon Kabat-Zinn got a PhD:** Mindful Staff, "Jon Kabat-Zinn, Advisory Board Member," Mindful, July 12, 2018, https://www .mindful.org/jon-kabat-zinn-advisory-board-member/.

159 **developed a skill called "STOP":** "Mindfulness STOP Skill," Cognitive Behavioral Therapy Los Angeles, March 26, 2022, https: //cogbtherapy.com/mindfulness-meditation-blog/mindfulness -stop-skill.

160 **"There are rare times":** Marty Nemko, MartyNemko.com, n.d., https://martynemko.com/articles/do-you-talk-too-much _id1371.

161 **Goulston calls momentum deafness:** Mark Goulston, "HBS—Just Listen," Mark Goulston, February 12, 2016, https: //markgoulston.com/how-well-do-you-listen-harvard-business -school-seems-to-think-not-well-enough/.

162 **"Keep it short and sweet":** "Tinder Founder Sean Rad's Top Tips for the Perfect Profile," *British GQ*, March 15, 2019, https: //www.gq-magazine.co.uk/article/tinder-perfect-profile-sean -rad#:~:text=We%20have%20a%20500%2Dcharacter,not%20 give%20too%20much%20away.

9: STFU IS POWER

163 **sends your email:** Shana Lebowitz and May Teng, "Anna Wintour's Strategy for Using Email to Get People to Confront Issues Sounds Terrifying—and Effective," *Business Insider*,

December 17, 2020, https://www.businessinsider.com/boss-people
-management-advice-empower-employees-vogue-anna-wintour.

163 **Wintour never puts a subject line**: Amy Odell, *Anna: The Biography* (New York: Gallery Books/Simon and Schuster, 2022), 3.

163 **adding just a single character**: Jeffrey Dastin, "With Bezos Out as Amazon CEO, Is This the End of His Ominous Question-Mark Emails?," Reuters, February 3, 2021, https://www.reuters .com/article/us-amazon-com-bezos/with-bezos-out-as-amazon -ceo-is-this-the-end-of-his-ominous-question-mark-emails -idUSKBN2A32Z8.

164 **reportedly has told employees**: Pauli Poisuo, "The Dark Truth About Amazon Founder Jeff Bezos," Grunge, May 18, 2022, https://www.grunge.com/143621/the-dark-truth-about-amazon -founder-jeff-bezos/.

164 **"Anna's power in those days"**: Odell, *Anna*, chap. 4.

165 **"I learned that you actually have more power"**: Nora McGreevy, "Hear an A.I.-Generated Andy Warhol 'Read' His Diary to You in New Documentary," *Smithsonian Magazine*, March 10, 2022, https://www.smithsonianmag.com/smart-news /an-ai-generated-andy-warhol-reads-his-diary-to-you-in-new -documentary-180979658/.

165 **Our brains crave the feeling**: David Robson, "How to Restore Your Sense of Control When You Feel Powerless," BBC Worklife, https://www.bbc.com/worklife/article/20201209-how-to-restore -your-sense-of-control-when-you-feel-powerless.

167 **Kawasaki says the perfect email**: Drake Baer, "Why Every Email Should Be 5 Sentences Long," Fast Company, July 26, 2013, https://www.fastcompany.com/3014857/why-every-email-should -be-5-sentences-long.

167 **average worker spends 28 percent**: Matt Plummer, "How to Spend Way Less Time on Email Every Day," *Harvard Business Review*, October 29, 2020, https://hbr.org/2019/01/how-to-spend -way-less-time-on-email-every-day.

169 **one of the first academics**: Bret Rappaport, "'Talk Less': Eloquent Silence in the Rhetoric of Lawyering," *Journal of Legal Education* 67, no. 1 (2017): 286–314, https://www.jstor.org/stable /26453545.

175 **"the godfather of the movie business"**: Jonathan Kandell, "Lew Wasserman, 89, Is Dead; Last of Hollywood's Moguls," *New York Times*, June 4, 2002, https://www.nytimes.com/2002/06/04/business /lew-wasserman-89-is-dead-last-of-hollywood-s-moguls.html.

175 *When Hollywood Had a King*: Connie Bruck, *When Hollywood Had a King: The Reign of Lew Wasserman Who Leveraged Talent into Power and Influence* (New York: Random House, 2004).

176 **"human verbal wrecking crew"**: John M. Broder, "Biden Living Up to His Gaffe-Prone Reputation," *New York Times*, September 11, 2008, https://www.nytimes.com/2008/09/11/world /americas/11iht-biden.4.16081515.html.

179 **"Throughout her career"**: George Packer, "The Quiet German: The Astonishing Rise of Angela Merkel, the Most Powerful Woman in the World," *New Yorker*, November 24, 2014, https: //www.newyorker.com/magazine/2014/12/01/quiet-german.

180 **she never used social media**: Franz Baumann, "Political Genius Flying at Low Altitude," *Los Angeles Review of Books*, October 30, 2021, https://lareviewofbooks.org/article/political -genius-flying-at-low-altitude/.

181 **Obama reportedly upset Merkel**: Alessandra Scotto di Santolo, "Revealed: Moment Barack Obama Made Angela Merkel Cry in Key Eurozone Crisis Meeting," *Express*, February 8, 2019, https://www.express.co.uk/news/world/1084075/EU-news -Angela-Merkel-Barack-Obama-G20-eurozone-crisis-Greece.

184 **Ginsburg decided to hold back**: Samantha Lachman and Ashley Alman, "Ruth Bader Ginsburg Reflects on a Polarizing Term One Month Out," *HuffPost*, July 29, 2015, https://www.huffpost.com /entry/ruth-bader-ginsburg-tk_n_55b97c68e4b0b8499b18536b.

186 **powerful people use more abstract language**: "You Look More Powerful When You Avoid Talking Details, Study Shows," Association for Psychological Science, July 11, 2014, https://www.psychologicalscience.org/news/minds-business/you-look-more-powerful-when-you-avoid-talking-details-study-shows.html.

187 **Leaving a brief pause**: Namkje Koudenburg, Tom Postmes, and Ernestine H. Gordijn, "Conversational Flow and Entitativity: The Role of Status," *British Journal of Social Psychology* 53, no. 2 (2013): 350–66, https://doi.org/10.1111/bjso.12027.

187 **use silence to signal disapproval**: Heidi Mitchell, "How to Use Silence in Business Meetings," *Wall Street Journal*, May 6, 2022, https://www.wsj.com/articles/use-silence-in-business-meetings-11651252991.

10: STFU AND LISTEN

191 **10 percent of the population**: Caren Osten, "Are You Really Listening, or Just Waiting to Talk?," *Psychology Today*, October 5, 2016, https://www.psychologytoday.com/us/blog/the-right-balance/201610/are-you-really-listening-or-just-waiting-talk.

191 **we retain only about 25 percent**: Stacey Hanke, "Are People Actually Listening to and Understanding What You Say? Here Are 5 Signs to Watch," *Entrepreneur*, October 26, 2017, https://www.entrepreneur.com/article/301188.

191 **humans speak about 125 words**: "Are You Really Listening: Hearing vs. Listening," Speakeasy, June 4, 2022, https://www.speakeasyinc.com/hearing-vs-listening/.

192 **brains are working overtime**: Manyu Jiang, "The Reason Zoom Calls Drain Your Energy," BBC Worklife, April 22, 2020, https://www.bbc.com/worklife/article/20200421-why-zoom-video-chats-are-so-exhausting.

194 **when doctors do not interrupt**: Danielle Ofri, "The Day

I Zipped My Lips and Let My Patients Talk," *First Opinion*, podcast, STAT, April 24, 2018, https://www.statnews.com/2017/02/07/let-patients-talk/.

194 **studies have found that empathic listening**: Danielle Ofri, "The Conversation Placebo," *New York Times*, January 19, 2017, https://www.nytimes.com/2017/01/19/opinion/sunday/the-conversation-placebo.html?_r=0.

195 **doctors come out of med school**: Helen Meldrum and Rebekah Apple, "Teaching or *Not* Teaching Empathic Listening to Future Physicians? Historical Roots and Ongoing Challenges," *International Journal of Listening* 35, no. 3 (2021): 209–15, https://doi.org/10.1080/10904018.2019.1684296.

196 **Wintour's biographer**: Odell, *Anna*, 309.

197 **"Can Anna Wintour Survive"**: Ginia Bellafante, "Can Anna Wintour Survive the Social Justice Movement?," *New York Times*, June 12, 2022, https://www.nytimes.com/2020/06/11/nyregion/anna-wintour-conde-nast-racism.html.

198 **been called the world's greatest leader**: "Tim Cook," *Fortune*, March 26, 2015, https://fortune.com/worlds-greatest-leaders/2015/tim-cook/.

201 **"you show up in a neighborhood"**: "Obama Promotes Listening Skills in First Public Appearance After Leaving Office," YouTube, April 24, 2017, https://www.youtube.com/watch?v=LQM5alO1rWs.

201 **a lot of successful entrepreneurs**: Louise Tickel, "Dyslexic Entrepreneurs—Why They Have a Competitive Edge," *Guardian*, January 15, 2015, https://www.theguardian.com/small-business-network/2015/jan/15/dyslexic-entrepreneurs-competitive-edge-business-leaders.

210 **no more phones or iPads**: Balazs Koranyi, Francesco Canepa, and Frank Siebelt, "No Phones, No Leaks: How Lagarde Is Making Her Mark on ECB," Reuters, February 10, 2020, https:

//www.reuters.com/article/us-ecb-policy-lagarde-inisght/no -phones-no-leaks-how-lagarde-is-making-her-mark-on-ecb -idUSKBN2040NO.

211 **More than half of communication:** "How to Use the 7–38–55 Rule to Negotiate Effectively."

ABOUT THE AUTHOR

Dan Lyons is the author of *Disrupted: My Adventures in the Start-Up Bubble*, a *New York Times* bestselling memoir, and *Lab Rats: How Silicon Valley Made Work Miserable for the Rest of Us*. He was also a writer for the hit HBO comedy series *Silicon Valley*. As a journalist, he spent a decade covering Silicon Valley for *Forbes*, ran tech coverage at *Newsweek*, and contributed to *Fortune*, the *New York Times*, *Wired*, *Vanity Fair*, and the *New Yorker*. In promoting the gospel of silence, he plans to scorn his own good advice as loudly as he can.